THE NEW
HEBREW THROUGH PRAYER

1

Terry Kaye

Contributing Authors:
Claudia Grossman
Lori Justice

BEHRMAN HOUSE, INC.

The publisher gratefully acknowledges the cooperation
of the following sources of photographs for this book:

Creative Image Photography 7, 31, 37, 63, 70, 76, 84, 94; NASA 22;
Francene Keery 12, 80; Bill Aron 43; Bev Weiss 55; Sunny Yellen, 58, 91
Cover: Beth Shepherd Peters

Book and Cover Design: Irving S. Berman
Electronic Composition and Page Production: 21st Century Publishing and Communications
Artists: Ilene Winn-Lederer (Chapter Openers); Deborah Zemke (Activity Art)

TABLE OF CONTENTS

בָּרְכוּ

What kinds of signals tell you something important is about to start? There's the bell announcing that it's time for recess, the ringing telephone meaning that someone wants to talk to you, and the lights going off in the movies telling you that the show is about to begin.

The בָּרְכוּ prayer is a signal—it calls the congregation together, announcing that the main part of the prayer service is about to start.

In many congregations the leader of the service says the first line of the בָּרְכוּ while bowing as a sign of respect to God—the same way one might bow down toward a king or a queen. The congregation recites the second line of the prayer in response while bowing, too.

Practice reading the בָּרְכוּ aloud.

1. בָּרְכוּ אֶת־יְיָ הַמְבֹרָךְ.

2. בָּרוּךְ יְיָ הַמְבֹרָךְ לְעוֹלָם וָעֶד.

Praise Adonai, who is to be praised.
Praised is Adonai, who is to be praised forever and ever.

PRAYER DICTIONARY

בָּרְכוּ
praise!

יְיָ
Adonai

הַמְבֹרָךְ
who is to be
praised

בָּרוּךְ
praised, blessed

לְעוֹלָם וָעֶד
forever and ever

SEARCH AND CIRCLE

Circle the Hebrew word(s) that means the same as the English.

forever and ever	אֶת וָעֶד לְעוֹלָם בָּרְכוּ
Adonai	יְיָ בָּרְכוּ בָּרוּךְ
praise!	אֶת הַמְבֹרָךְ בָּרְכוּ
who is to be praised	הַמְבֹרָךְ וָעֶד לְעוֹלָם אֶת

MATCH GAME

Connect the Hebrew word(s) to the English meaning.

who is to be praised   בָּרְכוּ

Adonai   יְיָ

praise!   הַמְבֹרָךְ

forever and ever   בָּרוּךְ

praised, blessed   לְעוֹלָם וָעֶד

WHAT'S MISSING?

Complete each prayer phrase with the missing Hebrew word(s).

אֶת יְיָ הַמְבֹרָךְ׃ _____ praise!

בָּרוּךְ יְיָ הַמְבֹרָךְ _____ _____ ׃ forever and ever

בָּרְכוּ אֶת _____ הַמְבֹרָךְ׃ Adonai

יְיָ הַמְבֹרָךְ לְעוֹלָם וָעֶד׃ _____ praised

FAMILY LETTERS

The words below contain family letters: כ כ ך and בּ ב.
Practice reading them.

כָּמוֹךָ	יָדְךָ	תּוֹכֵנוּ	לָךְ	כָּל	מֶלֶךְ	כ ך	.1
מְכַלְכֵּל	כְּמַלְכֵּנוּ	כָּמֹכָה	מִכָּל	אָכַל	כָּל	כ כ	.2
אֲבָל	כּוֹכָבִים	בִּדְבָרוֹ	בַּלֵּבָב	מַכַּבִּי	בְּבֵית	בּ ב	.3

6

IN THE SYNAGOGUE

How did the בָּרְכוּ get its name? בָּרְכוּ is the first word of the prayer. The first word of a Hebrew prayer is often the name by which the prayer is known.

The בָּרְכוּ is thousands of years old. The Jewish people have said the בָּרְכוּ since the time of the Temple—בֵּית הַמִּקְדָּשׁ. Today, in many congregations the leader of the service calls us to pray with the very same words that were recited in the Temple.

The cantor or rabbi chants

בָּרְכוּ אֶת־יְיָ הַמְבֹרָךְ.

and the congregation answers

בָּרוּךְ יְיָ הַמְבֹרָךְ לְעוֹלָם וָעֶד.

Just as we respond to a friendly "hello" with a greeting, we answer the בָּרְכוּ—the Call to Prayer—with the response that yes, we will pray.

7

TRUE OR FALSE

Put a ✔ next to each sentence that is *true*.

_____ The בָּרְכוּ is the Call to Prayer.

_____ A Hebrew prayer gets its name from the last word of the prayer.

_____ The בָּרְכוּ marks the start of the main part of the prayer service.

_____ The בָּרְכוּ is a new prayer.

_____ The בָּרְכוּ tells us to praise God.

DISCOVER THE PRAYER

Cross out every other letter in the design. Then read the prayer.

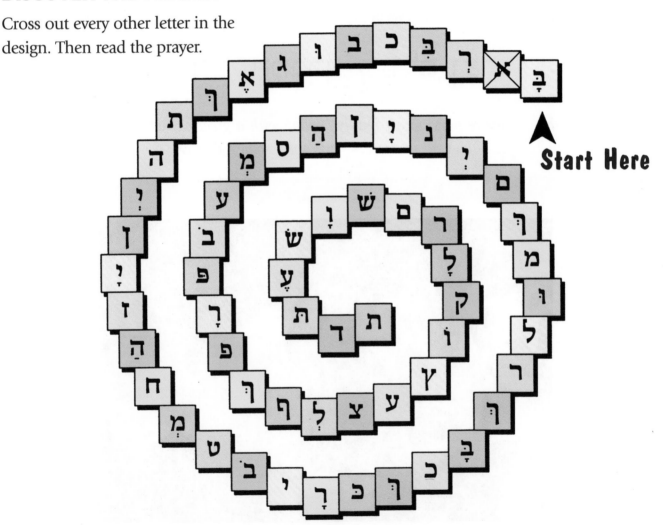

Start Here

8

ROOTS

Three words in the בָּרְכוּ look and sound similar.

בָּרְכוּ   הַמְבֹרָךְ   בָּרוּךְ

Which three letters appear in each word? _____ _____ _____

(Hint: ךּ כֹּ *and* בּ בֹּ *are family letters.)*

> Most Hebrew words are built on roots.
>
> A root usually consists of three letters that form the foundation for new, related words.
>
> A root has no vowels.
>
> The three words above share the root ברכ.
>
> The root ברכ means "bless" or "praise."

Circle the three root letters in each of these words:

בָּרוּךְ   בָּרְכוּ   הַמְבֹרָךְ

Write the root. _____ _____ _____

What does the root ברכ mean? _____ _____

FINAL LETTER REVIEW

The words below end in a final letter. Practice reading the words.

1. עֵץ   שָׁלוֹם   בָּרוּךְ   חָמֵץ   נוֹתֵן

2. יוֹסֵף   אַבְרָהָם   מִנְיָן   מֶלֶךְ   אָלֶף

9

DID YOU KNOW?

The בָּרְכוּ is also part of the blessing said before we read from the Torah.

Practice reading the Torah blessing.

1. בָּרְכוּ אֶת־יְיָ הַמְבֹרָךְ.

2. בָּרוּךְ יְיָ הַמְבֹרָךְ לְעוֹלָם וָעֶד.

3. בָּרוּךְ אַתָּה, יְיָ אֱלֹהֵינוּ, מֶלֶךְ הָעוֹלָם,

4. אֲשֶׁר בָּחַר בָּנוּ מִכָּל הָעַמִּים, וְנָתַן לָנוּ אֶת תּוֹרָתוֹ.

5. בָּרוּךְ אַתָּה, יְיָ, נוֹתֵן הַתּוֹרָה.

Why do you think the בָּרְכוּ was made a part of the Torah blessing?

_____

_____

_____

GOD'S NAME

God's true name is a mystery to us. A long time ago, the *kohanim*—the priests who served in the Temple in Jerusalem—knew how to pronounce God's name. But because it was so holy, the High Priest would say God's name only once a year—on Yom Kippur.

Today we are not really sure how God's name was pronounced, so we say Adonai. (Some people say הַשֵּׁם—The Name.)

We pronounce God's name יְיָ as אֲדוֹנָי.

God's name is written in many different ways.

In the בָּרְכוּ God's name is written יְיָ.

In other places in the סִדּוּר, and in the Bible (תַּנַ"ךְ), you may see God's name written יְהֹוָה. יְהֹוָה is also pronounced "Adonai."

In other Hebrew books you may see God's name written like this: ה'.

You will learn other names for God in later lessons.

READING PRACTICE

Practice reading the following sentences. Circle God's name wherever it appears.

1. בָּרְכוּ אֶת־יְיָ הַמְבֹרָךְ.

2. בָּרוּךְ יְיָ הַמְבֹרָךְ לְעוֹלָם וָעֶד.

3. מֵאֵין כָּמוֹךְ, יְהֹוָה, גָּדוֹל אַתָּה וְגָדוֹל שִׁמְךָ בִּגְבוּרָה.

4. כִּי לְךָ ה' הַגְּדֻלָה וְהַגְּבוּרָה וְהַתִּפְאֶרֶת.

5. יְיָ צְבָאוֹת שְׁמוֹ.

6. גָּדוֹל ה' וּמְהֻלָּל מְאֹד, וְלִגְדֻלָּתוֹ אֵין חֵקֶר.

11

HOW WOULD YOU RESPOND?

In the בָּרְכוּ the leader of the service *calls* us to pray. We *hear* and we *answer*: "Yes, we will pray."

In each example below, tell how you would respond.

<u>YOU HEAR:</u>	<u>YOU DO OR SAY:</u>
The doorbell ringing	_____
"Shabbat shalom"	_____
Mom calling	_____
A neighbor struggling with heavy packages	_____
Latkes sizzling in oil	_____
The blast of the shofar	_____
The alarm clock buzzing	_____
Haman's name	_____
בָּרְכוּ אֶת־יְיָ הַמְבֹרָךְ	_____

FLUENT READING

Practice reading the lines below.

١. בָּרְכוּ אֶת־יְיָ הַמְבֹרָךְ.

٢. בָּרוּךְ יְיָ הַמְבֹרָךְ לְעוֹלָם וָעֶד.

٣. בָּרוּךְ אַתָּה יְיָ הָאֵל הַקָּדוֹשׁ.

٤. יְיָ עֹז לְעַמּוֹ יִתֵּן, יְיָ יְבָרֵךְ אֶת עַמּוֹ בַשָּׁלוֹם.

٥. בָּרוּךְ אַתָּה, יְיָ, הַמְבָרֵךְ אֶת עַמּוֹ יִשְׂרָאֵל בַּשָּׁלוֹם.

٦. דָּבָר טוֹב וְקַיָּם לְעוֹלָם וָעֶד.

٧. תְּהִלּוֹת לְאֵל עֶלְיוֹן, בָּרוּךְ הוּא וּמְבֹרָךְ.

٨. יְיָ, צוּרִי וְגֹאֲלִי.

٩. בָּרֵךְ עָלֵינוּ, יְיָ אֱלֹהֵינוּ, אֶת הַשָּׁנָה הַזֹּאת.

מַעֲרִיב עֲרָבִים/
יוֹצֵר אוֹר

מַעֲרִיב עֲרָבִים

What's your favorite part of the day—morning or evening? Maybe you love the evening! The sun turns from yellow to red, the clouds turn pink, and a beautiful, deep blue-purple spreads across the sky. You can see the first stars start to twinkle as night moves in, and there's a feeling of calm and peace, as if the whole world were settling down to rest. The מַעֲרִיב עֲרָבִים prayer is said every day as daylight turns to evening. It praises God for creating the twilight and the darkness—every single day.

Practice reading these lines from מַעֲרִיב עֲרָבִים.

1. בָּרוּךְ אַתָּה, יְיָ אֱלֹהֵינוּ, מֶלֶךְ הָעוֹלָם,
אֲשֶׁר בִּדְבָרוֹ מַעֲרִיב עֲרָבִים.

2. אֵל חַי וְקַיָּם, תָּמִיד יִמְלֹךְ עָלֵינוּ, לְעוֹלָם וָעֶד.
בָּרוּךְ אַתָּה, יְיָ, הַמַּעֲרִיב עֲרָבִים.

Praised are You, Adonai our God, Ruler of the world, whose word brings on the evening.

May the living and eternal God rule over us always. Praised are You, Adonai, who brings on the evening.

מַעֲרִיב עֲרָבִים

brings on the evening

חַי

living, lives

וְקַיָּם

and eternal

יִמְלֹךְ

will rule

WORD MATCH

Connect the English words to the matching Hebrew.

living, lives   מַעֲרִיב עֲרָבִים

will rule   חַי

brings on the evening   וְקַיָּם

and eternal   יִמְלֹךְ

COMPLETE THE PHRASE

Fill in the missing word.

מַעֲרִיב _____

brings on the _____

SING ALONG!

Do you know this song?

דָּוִד מֶלֶךְ יִשְׂרָאֵל חַי וְקַיָּם.

Circle the words in the song that also appear in the
מַעֲרִיב עֲרָבִים prayer.

IN THE SYNAGOGUE

מַעֲרִיב עֲרָבִים is said before the *evening* Shema prayer; it has a "partner prayer" that is said before the *morning* Shema. You will learn about the partner prayer—יוֹצֵר אוֹר—in the second part of this chapter, and you will learn about the Shema itself in the next chapter.

יוֹצֵר אוֹר and מַעֲרִיב עֲרָבִים are linked because they remind us that God creates both morning and night, light and darkness. And we praise God for bringing us morning after night after morning . . . day after day after day.

Why do you think we need to say a prayer praising God's creations both in the evening and in the morning?

READING PRACTICE

Practice reading the words below. Watch for the differences between **ע** and **צ**!

1. צִיצִית   מַעֲרִיב   מַצָּה   עִבְרִית   מִצְוָה   עֶרֶב

2. עֲרָבִים   עֲבוֹדָה   הַמּוֹצִיא   צְדָקָה   הָעֵץ   צַדִּיק

tree   *work עֲבוֹדָה*

16

ROOTS

Two words in מַעֲרִיב עֲרָבִים look and sound similar.

מַעֲרִיב   עֲרָבִים

> Most Hebrew words are built on roots.
> A root usually consists of three letters.
>
> The two words above share the root ערב.
> ערב means "evening."
>
> Write the root. _____ _____ _____
>
> What does the root ערב mean? _____

Circle the two words with the root ערב—"evening"—in each sentence below.

1. בָּרוּךְ אַתָּה, יְיָ אֱלֹהֵינוּ, מֶלֶךְ הָעוֹלָם, אֲשֶׁר בִּדְבָרוֹ
   מַעֲרִיב עֲרָבִים . . .

2. בָּרוּךְ אַתָּה, יְיָ, הַמַּעֲרִיב עֲרָבִים.

Think About This!

Why do you think the prayer begins *and* ends with the statement that God brings on the evening—מַעֲרִיב עֲרָבִים?

יוֹצֵר אוֹר

Maybe you love the daytime. One of the best things about the morning is that it means a new chance to have fun, to learn, and to do something special. Maybe there's a new kid at school you've been waiting to meet, or a soccer match after school. The יוֹצֵר אוֹר prayer is said every morning to praise God for creating the morning light, for giving us renewed energy, and for bringing us the blessing of another day to do good things.

Practice reading these lines from יוֹצֵר אוֹר.

1. בָּרוּךְ אַתָּה, יְיָ אֱלֹהֵינוּ, מֶלֶךְ הָעוֹלָם, יוֹצֵר אוֹר וּבוֹרֵא חֹשֶׁךְ, עֹשֶׂה שָׁלוֹם וּבוֹרֵא אֶת הַכֹּל.

2. בָּרוּךְ אַתָּה, יְיָ, יוֹצֵר הַמְּאוֹרוֹת.

Praised are You, Adonai our God, Ruler of the world, who forms light and creates darkness, who makes peace and creates all things.

Praised are You, Adonai, who forms the lights.

יוֹצֵר	forms
אוֹר	light
וּבוֹרֵא	and creates
חֹשֶׁךְ	darkness
עֹשֶׂה	makes
שָׁלוֹם	peace
הַכֹּל	all things, everything

PHRASE MATCH

Connect each Hebrew phrase to the matching English.

and creates all things   יוֹצֵר אוֹר

makes peace   וּבוֹרֵא חֹשֶׁךְ

forms light   עֹשֶׂה שָׁלוֹם

and creates darkness   וּבוֹרֵא אֶת הַכֹּל

WHAT'S MISSING?

Fill in the missing Hebrew word in each phrase.

1. וּבוֹרֵא _____
   and creates *darkness*

2. _____ אֶת הַכֹּל
   and creates all things

3. יוֹצֵר _____
   forms *light*

4. עֹשֶׂה _____
   makes *peace*

CREATION CONTINUES

Both יוֹצֵר אוֹר and מַעֲרִיב עֲרָבִים praise God, the Creator, and describe some of the things that God creates.

This is what יוֹצֵר אוֹר and מַעֲרִיב עֲרָבִים say God does:

1. מַעֲרִיב עֲרָבִים
brings on the evening

2. יוֹצֵר אוֹר
forms light

3. בּוֹרֵא חשֶׁךְ
creates darkness

4. עשֶׂה שָׁלוֹם
makes peace

5. בּוֹרֵא אֶת הַכּל
creates all things

Why do you think the prayers include so many words that mean "create"? What does that tell us about God?

It tills us that God
Created a lot of thing

A DOUBLE-DUTY DOT

Sometimes the dot for שׁ (shin) and שׂ (sin) identifies the letter *and* the vowel "וֹ".

Read each word below.

חשֶׁךְ שָׁלשׁ משֶׁה וַיֶּחֱשׂף קָדשׁ

20

IN THE SYNAGOGUE

There are *two* blessings before the Shema prayer, which you will learn about in the next chapter. Each blessing has an *evening* and a *morning* version. You have already learned the first blessing before the Shema.

First blessing before the Shema

This blessing celebrates the wonder of creation and its renewal each day.

Evening blessing: מַעֲרִיב עֲרָבִים

Morning blessing: יוֹצֵר אוֹר

We also say a second blessing before the Shema.

Second blessing before the Shema

This blessing thanks God for giving us the Torah and mitzvot and—in this way—for showing us love.

Evening blessing: אַהֲבַת עוֹלָם

Morning blessing: אַהֲבָה רַבָּה

After the Shema comes the Ve'ahavta prayer—when we declare *our* love for *God*!

Think About This!

Why do you think we need to declare *our* love for God after describing God's love for *us*?

DRAW THE TIME

Draw a moon and stars above the name of the creation blessing we say at night.

Draw a sun above the name of the creation blessing we say in the morning.

יוֹצֵר אוֹר   מַעֲרִיב עֲרָבִים

A COMMON WORD

אוֹר   means   "light."

הַמְּאוֹרוֹת   means   "the lights."

Circle אוֹר within the word הַמְּאוֹרוֹת.

What are "the lights" that God creates each day?

_____

THINK ABOUT THIS!

Which word or phrase do you consider to be the most important in מַעֲרִיב עֲרָבִים? Write it here. _____

Which word or phrase do you consider to be the most important in יוֹצֵר אוֹר? Write it here. _____

Why did you choose these words or phrases?

FLUENT READING

Practice reading the lines below.

1. וַיְהִי עֶרֶב וַיְהִי בֹקֶר.

2. וְעַל־מְאוֹרֵי־אוֹר שֶׁעָשִׂיתָ.

3. הַמֵּאִיר לָאָרֶץ וְלַדָּרִים עָלֶיהָ בְּרַחֲמִים.

4. עֹשֶׂה שָׁלוֹם וּבוֹרֵא אֶת־הַכֹּל.

5. וַיְכַל אֱלֹהִים בַּיּוֹם הַשְּׁבִיעִי מְלַאכְתּוֹ אֲשֶׁר עָשָׂה.

6. הָעֹשֶׂה גְדֹלוֹת עַד אֵין חֵקֶר.

7. בּוֹרֵא יוֹם וָלָיְלָה, גּוֹלֵל אוֹר מִפְּנֵי חֹשֶׁךְ וְחֹשֶׁךְ מִפְּנֵי אוֹר.

8. אֱמֶת וֶאֱמוּנָה כָּל־זֹאת, וְקַיָּם עָלֵינוּ כִּי הוּא יְיָ אֱלֹהֵינוּ.

9. בָּרוּךְ אַתָּה, יְיָ אֱלֹהֵינוּ, מֶלֶךְ הָעוֹלָם, בּוֹרֵא מְאוֹרֵי הָאֵשׁ.

10. וּמַעֲבִיר יוֹם וּמֵבִיא לָיְלָה, וּמַבְדִּיל בֵּין יוֹם וּבֵין לָיְלָה.

שְׁמַע

The שְׁמַע expresses a feeling and a belief so strong it is unlike anything else—and so deeply felt that there are almost no words to describe it. This prayer is our pledge of loyalty to God; when we say it, we are expressing our belief in only one God who created the entire universe. The שְׁמַע expresses the very core of our faith. It is such an important and intense prayer that many people recite it with their eyes closed so they can concentrate completely on this pledge. The first line of the שְׁמַע declares our belief in one God; the second line praises God's name.

The first line of the שְׁמַע is said in a loud and clear voice.

שְׁמַע יִשְׂרָאֵל: יְיָ אֱלֹהֵינוּ, יְיָ אֶחָד.

Hear O Israel: Adonai is our God, Adonai is One.

These words come from the Book of Deuteronomy in the Bible. They became part of our prayer service about 2,000 years ago.

שְׁמַע
hear

יִשְׂרָאֵל
Israel

יְיָ
Adonai

אֱלֹהֵינוּ
our God

אֶחָד
one

WHAT'S MISSING?

Complete each prayer phrase with the missing English word.

שְׁמַע   _____ O Israel

אֶחָד   Adonai is _____

יִשְׂרָאֵל   Hear O _____

יְיָ   _____ is our God

UNSCRAMBLE THE PRAYER

Put the שְׁמַע in the correct order by numbering the words from 1 to 6.

יְיָ יִשְׂרָאֵל שְׁמַע אֶחָד אֱלֹהֵינוּ יְיָ

( ) ( ) ( ) (1) ( ) ( )

Think About This!

In ancient times, Jews recited the שְׁמַע, declaring their belief in only one God—even while many other people believed in many gods, for example, a sun god, a moon god, a god of life, and others. It was not easy for the Jewish people to be true to their belief when everyone else felt otherwise. Have you ever been in a situation where your opinion was different from everyone else's but you stuck to it anyway? Why was it important to you?

An Ethical Echo

The שְׁמַע prayer speaks directly to us. We are עַם יִשְׂרָאֵל—the people of Israel. יִשְׂרָאֵל is also part of the full name of the State of Israel: מְדִינַת יִשְׂרָאֵל. So the name can refer both to the Jewish people and to the modern state of Israel. In the שְׁמַע, the word refers to Jewish people everywhere, whether they live in Israel or around the world.

The Jewish people have an expression that all of יִשְׂרָאֵל is responsible for one another:

כָּל יִשְׂרָאֵל עֲרֵבִים זֶה בָּזֶה.

Think About This!

Why is it especially important for the Jewish people to be responsible for one another?

FAMILY LETTERS

The words below contain the family letters שׁ and שׂ.
Practice reading the words.

שֵׁשֶׁת	שֵׁשׁ	שֵׁם	שְׁמוֹ	שָׁמַע	שָׁלוֹם	.1
שַׁעֲשָׂה	יִשְׂרָאֵל	עָשָׂה	שָׁם	שְׂאוּ	שָׂשׂוֹן	.2
מֹשֶׁה	לַעֲשׂוֹת	רֹאשׁ	שָׁלֹשׁ	שִׂים	שָׂמֵחַ	.3

26

Prayer Building Blocks

אֱלֹהֵינוּ "our God"

The word אֱלֹהֵינוּ is made up of two parts:

אֱלֹהֵי means "God of."

נוּ is an ending that means "us" or "our."

אֱלֹהֵינוּ means "our God."

Circle the Hebrew word that means "our God" in the following prayer:

שְׁמַע יִשְׂרָאֵל: יְיָ אֱלֹהֵינוּ, יְיָ אֶחָד.

Write the ending that means "us" or "our." _____ .

Write the Hebrew word that means "our God." _____ .

Because our ancestors were the first to know that God is the One God of all the world, we feel especially close to God—and so we say *our God.*

READING PRACTICE

Practice reading the following סִדּוּר phrases.

Circle the word אֱלֹהֵינוּ wherever it appears.

1. רְצֵה יְיָ אֱלֹהֵינוּ בְּעַמְּךָ יִשְׂרָאֵל.

2. בָּרֵךְ עָלֵינוּ, יְיָ אֱלֹהֵינוּ, אֶת הַשָּׁנָה הַזֹּאת.

3. אַהֲבָה רַבָּה אֲהַבְתָּנוּ, יְיָ אֱלֹהֵינוּ.

4. הַשְׁכִּיבֵנוּ יְיָ אֱלֹהֵינוּ לְשָׁלוֹם.

In each of the sentences above, the Hebrew word for Adonai also appears. Write the Hebrew word for Adonai. _____

27

THE RESPONSE

The line following the שְׁמַע is spoken quietly.

בָּרוּךְ שֵׁם כְּבוֹד מַלְכוּתוֹ לְעוֹלָם וָעֶד.

Blessed is the name of God's glorious kingdom forever and ever.

These words are not from the Bible. They were first recited in the ancient Temple in Jerusalem. They later became the *response*, or follow-up, to the first line of the שְׁמַע prayer.

. . . .

Practice reading the שְׁמַע aloud.

1. שְׁמַע יִשְׂרָאֵל: יְיָ אֱלֹהֵינוּ, יְיָ אֶחָד.

2. בָּרוּךְ שֵׁם כְּבוֹד מַלְכוּתוֹ לְעוֹלָם וָעֶד.

DID YOU KNOW?

Many congregations say the second line of the שְׁמַע in a quiet voice. Why?

Our tradition tells us that during the time when the Roman Empire ruled the Land of Israel, it was forbidden to praise any kings other than the Roman emperors. Rome sent spies to the synagogues to listen to the prayers, so the Jews would whisper the words that praised God as Ruler forever and ever.

Can you think of another example of people who might have to whisper to protect themselves?

בָּרוּךְ

blessed, praised

שֵׁם

name

כְּבוֹד

glory of

מַלְכוּתוֹ

God's kingdom

לְעוֹלָם וָעֶד

forever and ever

WHAT'S MISSING?

Complete each prayer phrase with the missing Hebrew word(s).

name   בָּרוּךְ _____ כְּבוֹד

forever and ever   מַלְכוּתוֹ _____ _____

blessed   שֵׁם כְּבוֹד _____

God's kingdom   כְּבוֹד _____ לְעוֹלָם וָעֶד

WORD MATCH

Match the English word(s) to the Hebrew meaning.

A. forever and ever   ( ) בָּרוּךְ

B. blessed   ( ) שֵׁם

C. God's kingdom   ( ) כְּבוֹד

D. name   ( ) מַלְכוּתוֹ

E. glory of   ( ) לְעוֹלָם וָעֶד

An Ethical Echo

Read these lines from Pirke Avot:

There are three crowns: the crown of Torah, the crown of priesthood, and the crown of royalty. But the crown of a good name— שֵׁם טוֹב *— excels them all.*

Think About This!

What does it mean to have a "good name"—שֵׁם טוֹב? What can you do to ensure your own good name?

Prayer Building Blocks

מַלְכוּתוֹ — "God's kingdom"

The word מַלְכוּתוֹ appears in the second line of the שְׁמַע.

The word מַלְכוּתוֹ is made up of two parts.

מַלְכוּת means "kingdom."

וֹ is an ending that means "his."

מַלְכוּתוֹ means "His kingdom" or "God's kingdom."

As God is neither male nor female, we translate the word מַלְכוּתוֹ as "God's kingdom."

Circle the word that means "God's kingdom" in the following prayer:

בָּרוּךְ שֵׁם כְּבוֹד מַלְכוּתוֹ לְעוֹלָם וָעֶד.

Write the Hebrew word that means "God's kingdom." _____

ROOTS

מַלְכוּתוֹ is built on the root מלכ.

The root מלכ means "rule." The three letters מלכ tell us that "king" or "ruler" is part of a word's meaning.

Circle the three root letters in this word.

מַלְכוּתוֹ

Write the root. _____ _____ _____

What does the root mean? _____

Read these words aloud. Circle the three root letters in each word.

יִמְלֹךְ   מַלְכָּה   מַלְכוּת   מַלְכֵּנוּ   מֶלֶךְ

BE A WITNESS

When we see the שְׁמַע in its source—the Torah scroll—we notice something very interesting. The last letter of the word שְׁמַע, ע, and the last letter of the word אֶחָד, ד, are written larger than all of the other letters.

שְׁמַע יִשְׂרָאֵל: יְהוָֹה אֱלֹהֵינוּ, יְהוָֹה אֶחָד.

These two letters together—עד—mean "witness." One of the lessons of the שְׁמַע is that each Jew has the potential to be a witness to the oneness and uniqueness of God.

What does it mean to be a witness to the fact that God is One?

TRUE OR FALSE

Put a ✔ next to each sentence that is true.

_____ The שְׁמַע commands us to "hear" an important statement about God.

_____ The שְׁמַע comes from the Book of Genesis in the Torah.

_____ In the שְׁמַע, we declare that we believe in one God.

_____ There are many prayers that are more important than the שְׁמַע.

_____ The first line of the שְׁמַע is said in a loud voice.

_____ The second line of the שְׁמַע comes from the Bible.

_____ We say the second line of the שְׁמַע in a soft voice.

FLUENT READING

Practice reading the lines below.

1. שְׁמַע יִשְׂרָאֵל: יְיָ אֱלֹהֵינוּ, יְיָ אֶחָד.

2. בָּרוּךְ שֵׁם כְּבוֹד מַלְכוּתוֹ לְעוֹלָם וָעֶד.

3. הַלְלוּ, עַבְדֵי יְיָ, הַלְלוּ אֶת שֵׁם יְיָ.

4. וְהוּא אֶחָד, וְאֵין שֵׁנִי.

5. בַּיּוֹם הַהוּא יִהְיֶה יְיָ אֶחָד וּשְׁמוֹ אֶחָד.

6. לֹא תִשָּׂא אֶת שֵׁם יְהוָה אֱלֹהֶיךָ לַשָּׁוְא.

7. צוּר יִשְׂרָאֵל, קוּמָה בְּעֶזְרַת יִשְׂרָאֵל.

8. שְׁמַע! בַּיָּמִים הָהֵם בַּזְּמַן הַזֶּה.

9. וְטוֹב וְיָפֶה הַדָּבָר הַזֶּה עָלֵינוּ לְעוֹלָם וָעֶד.

10. אַהֲבָה רַבָּה אֲהַבְתָּנוּ, יְיָ אֱלֹהֵינוּ.

11. וַיְהִי עֶרֶב וַיְהִי בֹקֶר, יוֹם אֶחָד.

וְאָהַבְתָּ

How do you show your parents that you love them? You might bring Dad breakfast in bed or help Mom weed the garden. Another important way to demonstrate your love for your parents is to show respect for them. The וְאָהַבְתָּ prayer reminds us to love God by respecting and following God's commandments. We put a mezuzah—a small box containing the words of the שְׁמַע and וְאָהַבְתָּ—on the doorposts of our house. Each time we look at the mezuzah it reminds us of our love for God and of our respect for God's commandments. וְאָהַבְתָּ comes immediately after the שְׁמַע in the siddur.

Practice reading the וְאָהַבְתָּ.

1. וְאָהַבְתָּ אֵת יְיָ אֱלֹהֶיךָ

2. בְּכָל־לְבָבְךָ וּבְכָל־נַפְשְׁךָ וּבְכָל־מְאֹדֶךָ.

3. וְהָיוּ הַדְּבָרִים הָאֵלֶּה, אֲשֶׁר אָנֹכִי מְצַוְּךָ הַיּוֹם, עַל־לְבָבֶךָ.

4. וְשִׁנַּנְתָּם לְבָנֶיךָ, וְדִבַּרְתָּ בָּם בְּשִׁבְתְּךָ בְּבֵיתֶךָ,

5. וּבְלֶכְתְּךָ בַדֶּרֶךְ, וּבְשָׁכְבְּךָ וּבְקוּמֶךָ.

6. וּקְשַׁרְתָּם לְאוֹת עַל־יָדֶךָ, וְהָיוּ לְטֹטָפֹת בֵּין עֵינֶיךָ.

7. וּכְתַבְתָּם עַל־מְזֻזוֹת בֵּיתֶךָ וּבִשְׁעָרֶיךָ.

You shall love Adonai, your God,
with all your heart, and with all your soul, and with all your might.
Set these words, which I command you this day, upon your heart.
Teach them to your children, and speak of them when you are at home,
and when you go on your way, and when you lie down, and when you get up.
Bind them as a sign upon your hand and let them be symbols between your eyes.
Write them on the doorposts of your house and on your gates.

34

PRAYER DICTIONARY

וְאָהַבְתָּ
you shall love

לְבָבְךָ
your heart

הַדְּבָרִים
the words

לְאוֹת
as a sign

מְזֻזוֹת
mezuzot

בֵּיתֶךָ
your house

NOTE THE NUMBER

In the circle below each Hebrew word write the number of the English translation.

לְבָבְךָ ⃝   מְזֻזוֹת ⃝   לְאוֹת ⃝

בֵּיתֶךָ ⃝   וְאָהַבְתָּ ⃝   הַדְּבָרִים ⃝

1. you shall love
2. the words
3. mezuzot
4. your house
5. as a sign
6. your heart

DRAW AND WRITE

Draw a picture to illustrate these words.

_____ 1. לְבָבְךָ

_____ 2. מְזֻזוֹת

_____ 3. בֵּיתֶךָ

Write the meaning of these words.

_____ 1. וְאָהַבְתָּ

_____ 2. הַדְּבָרִים

_____ 3. לְאוֹת

ROOTS

The theme of וְאָהַבְתָּ is our love for God. Look at the names of these three prayers having to do with the love between God and the Jewish people.

וְאָהַבְתָּ   אַהֲבַת עוֹלָם   אַהֲבָה רַבָּה

Do you notice a common root?

The root אהב means *love*.

Circle the three root letters—אהב—in each word below.

וְאָהַבְתָּ   אַהֲבַת   אַהֲבָה

Write the root. _____ _____ _____

What does the root mean? _____

Read the following prayer excerpts and circle all the words with the root אהב.

1. הַבּוֹחֵר בְּעַמּוֹ יִשְׂרָאֵל בְּאַהֲבָה
2. אַהֲבַת עוֹלָם בֵּית יִשְׂרָאֵל עַמְּךָ אָהַבְתָּ
3. וְיַחֵד לְבָבֵנוּ לְאַהֲבָה וּלְיִרְאָה אֶת שְׁמֶךָ
4. בְּאַהֲבָה וּבְרָצוֹן שַׁבַּת קָדְשֶׁךָ
5. אַהֲבָה רַבָּה אֲהַבְתָּנוּ יְיָ אֱלֹהֵינוּ
6. כָּל דִּבְרֵי תַלְמוּד תּוֹרָתֶךָ בְּאַהֲבָה

וְאָהַבְתָּ tells us to reciprocate God's love for us. Write one way that we can show our love for God.

_____

_____

Prayer Building Blocks

הַדְּבָרִים "the words"

הַדְּבָרִים means "the words."

הַדְּבָרִים is made up of two parts:

הַ means "the."

דְּבָרִים means "words."

Circle the word part that means "the." הַדְּבָרִים

Write the word part that means "the." _____

An Ethical Echo

In the Jewish tradition there is a saying that *Talmud Torah* (תַּלְמוּד תּוֹרָה)—the Study of the Torah—is more important than anything:

תַּלְמוּד תּוֹרָה כְּנֶגֶד כֻּלָם.

Since both the שְׁמַע and the וְאָהַבְתָּ prayers are taken from the Torah, when you say these prayers you are studying the Torah. So reciting the שְׁמַע actually helps you fulfill the mitzvah it asks you to do!

Think About This!

It is not enough just to *study* the Torah; it is just as important to *do* Torah (perform God's mitzvot).

Why do you think that studying the Torah and fulfilling its commandments are both elements of *Talmud Torah*? How do they help you to be a better person?

READING PRACTICE

Sometimes the vowel ָ has the sound of the vowel "וֹ." Practice reading the words and phrases below.

1. בְּכָל לְבָבְךָ   כָּל   קָדְשְׁךָ   אָזְנַיִם

2. וּבְשָׁכְבְּךָ   וּבְכָל נַפְשְׁךָ   שֶׁבְּכָל הַלֵּילוֹת

38

Prayer Building Blocks

בֵּיתֶךָ "your house"

The word בֵּיתֶךָ is made up of two parts:

בַּיִת means "house."

ךָ is an ending that means "you" or "your."

בֵּיתֶךָ means "your house."

(When we combine בַּיִת and ךָ, the word is written בֵּיתֶךָ or בֵּיתְךָ.)

There are many words in the וְאָהַבְתָּ with the ending ךָ.

Read the first three lines of the וְאָהַבְתָּ and circle each word with the ending ךָ.

1. וְאָהַבְתָּ אֵת יְיָ אֱלֹהֶיךָ

2. בְּכָל־לְבָבְךָ וּבְכָל־נַפְשְׁךָ וּבְכָל־מְאֹדֶךָ.

3. וְהָיוּ הַדְּבָרִים הָאֵלֶּה, אֲשֶׁר אָנֹכִי מְצַוְּךָ הַיּוֹם,
עַל־לְבָבֶךָ.

How many words did you circle? _____

What does the ending ךָ mean? _____ _____

Whom is the prayer addressing?

_____

BACK TO THE SOURCES

This is a page from the Book of Deuteronomy. In this selection Moses talks to the Children of Israel about how they should behave when they enter the land of Canaan.

Can you find and read the שְׁמַע?

Can you find and read the וְאָהַבְתָּ?

Can you find the two larger letters (עד)? What do they mean when combined to form one word?

4 ה שְׁמַע יִשְׂרָאֵל יְהֹוָה אֱלֹהֵינוּ יְהֹוָה ׀ אֶחָד: וְאָהַבְתָּ אֵת
יְהֹוָה אֱלֹהֶיךָ בְּכָל־לְבָבְךָ וּבְכָל־נַפְשְׁךָ וּבְכָל־מְאֹדֶךָ:
6 וְהָיוּ הַדְּבָרִים הָאֵלֶּה אֲשֶׁר אָנֹכִי מְצַוְּךָ הַיּוֹם עַל־לְבָבֶךָ:
7 וְשִׁנַּנְתָּם לְבָנֶיךָ וְדִבַּרְתָּ בָּם בְּשִׁבְתְּךָ בְּבֵיתֶךָ וּבְלֶכְתְּךָ
8 בַדֶּרֶךְ וּבְשָׁכְבְּךָ וּבְקוּמֶךָ: וּקְשַׁרְתָּם לְאוֹת עַל־יָדֶךָ וְהָיוּ
9 לְטֹטָפֹת בֵּין עֵינֶיךָ: וּכְתַבְתָּם עַל־מְזֻזוֹת בֵּיתֶךָ וּבִשְׁעָרֶיךָ:

FLUENT READING

Some congregations add these words after the וְאָהַבְתָּ.
Practice reading the lines below.

1. לְמַעַן תִּזְכְּרוּ וַעֲשִׂיתֶם אֶת־כָּל־מִצְוֹתָי, וִהְיִיתֶם קְדֹשִׁים

2. לֵאלֹהֵיכֶם. אֲנִי יְיָ אֱלֹהֵיכֶם, אֲשֶׁר הוֹצֵאתִי אֶתְכֶם מֵאֶרֶץ

3. מִצְרַיִם לִהְיוֹת לָכֶם לֵאלֹהִים. אֲנִי יְיָ אֱלֹהֵיכֶם.

The blessing that follows after the שְׁמַע is called the גְּאֻלָּה—Redemption.
It praises God for saving us from slavery in Egypt. You'll learn more about
the song at the heart of the גְּאֻלָּה in the next chapter.

Meanwhile, practice reading these lines from the גְּאֻלָּה.

1. אֱמֶת וְיַצִּיב, וְאָהוּב וְחָבִיב, וְנוֹרָא וְאַדִּיר.

2. מִמִּצְרַיִם גְּאַלְתָּנוּ, יְיָ אֱלֹהֵינוּ, וּמִבֵּית עֲבָדִים פְּדִיתָנוּ.

3. תְּהִלּוֹת לְאֵל עֶלְיוֹן, בָּרוּךְ הוּא וּמְבֹרָךְ. מֹשֶׁה וּבְנֵי

4. יִשְׂרָאֵל לְךָ עָנוּ שִׁירָה בְּשִׂמְחָה רַבָּה, וְאָמְרוּ כֻלָּם:

Now turn to Chapter 5 for the song at the
heart of the מִי כָמֹכָה—גְּאֻלָּה!

מִי כָמֹכָה

Are there things you have seen or experienced that have left you in awe, wondering how they could possibly happen? Things that seemed impossible but somehow happened anyway? Some people call these kinds of experiences "miracles." The מִי כָמֹכָה prayer was first said by the Jews who were slaves in Egypt when they observed the miraculous parting of the Sea of Reeds, which allowed them to escape to freedom. They said the מִי כָמֹכָה—meaning "Who is like You?"—in praise of God and in acknowledgment of God's unique and awesome power in setting them free.

Practice reading מִי כָמֹכָה aloud.

1. מִי־כָמֹכָה בָּאֵלִם, יְיָ?

2. מִי כָּמֹכָה, נֶאְדָּר בַּקֹדֶשׁ,

3. נוֹרָא תְהִלֹת, עֹשֵׂה פֶלֶא?

Who is like You among the gods [other nations worship], Adonai?
Who is like You, majestic in (the) holiness,
Awesome in splendor, doing wonders?

THINK ABOUT THIS!

What kinds of nearly impossible events or actions have you observed? What made them seem impossible, and how do you think they occurred? Do you think they were miracles?

מִי

who

כָּמֹכָה, כָּמֹכָה

like You

בָּאֵלִם

among the gods
[other nations worship]

יְיָ

Adonai

נֶאְדָּר

majestic

בַּקֹּדֶשׁ

in (the) holiness

SEARCH AND CIRCLE

Circle the Hebrew word or phrase that means the same as the English.

like You	סִדּוּר	כָּמֹכָה	שְׁמַע
Adonai	מִי	בָּאֵלִם	יְיָ
majestic	יִשְׂרָאֵל	בַּקֹּדֶשׁ	נֶאְדָּר
who	מִי	אֶחָד	שֵׁם
in (the) holiness	בָּרְכוּ	בַּקֹּדֶשׁ	בָּאֵלִם
among the gods [other nations worship]	בָּאֵלִם	הַמְבֹרָךְ	לְעוֹלָם וָעֶד

מִי־כָמֹכָה בָּאֵלִם, יְיָ?

מִי כָּמֹכָה, נֶאְדָּר בַּקֹּדֶשׁ.

1. Underline the words that mean "who is like You."

2. Draw a star over the Hebrew word for "in (the) holiness."

3. Circle the word that means "among the gods [other nations worship]."

4. Draw a squiggly line under the word that means "majestic."

5. Draw a triangle around the Hebrew word for "Adonai."

6. Write the two similar words that appear in both lines.

_____

7. What is the English meaning of these two words?

_____

IMAGINE THAT!

The word בָּאֵלִם ("among the gods") is misspelled in the מִי כָמֹכָה. The י before the מ is left out. The rabbis explain that this misspelling suggests that the other gods are false gods—they don't really exist. יְיָ is the one, true God.

THE HOLIDAY CONNECTION

Legend has it that in order to gather the Jews to fight their enemy King Antiochus in ancient days, the Jewish leader, Judah, called out the first words of the מִי כָמֹכָה. The first letters of these words then became the freedom fighters' name—the Maccabees. We celebrate the victory of the Maccabees in winning religious freedom on Ḥanukkah. And some people believe that the story of Ḥanukkah—where one little pitcher of olive oil provided enough oil for the menorah to be lighted for eight long days— is another miracle!

··

Write the first letter of each Hebrew word in the spaces below.

מִי כָמֹכָה בָּאֵלִם יְיָ

_____ _____ _____ _____

What does this word spell? _____

Why do you think Judah chose this prayer to rally the Jews together?

_____

_____

An Ethical Echo

Throughout the ages the Jewish people have experienced captivity and freedom, slavery and independence. We know how precious freedom is. And we are determined to rescue those who are not free.

We call this the mitzvah of *Pidyon Shevuyim*— פִּדְיוֹן שְׁבוּיִים—Redeeming Captives.

Think About This!

In what ways do we try to bring freedom to other people in the world?

IN THE SYNAGOGUE

The prayer מִי כָמֹכָה is from the Torah. It appears in the Book of Exodus. Exodus tells the story of our people's journey from slavery in Egypt to freedom. מִי כָמֹכָה appears in the Torah after the Children of Israel have safely crossed the Sea of Reeds.

Today, מִי כָמֹכָה is read at both the morning and evening services in the synagogue.

....

Practice reading מִי כָמֹכָה.

Who is like You among the gods
[other nations worship], Adonai?

1. מִי־כָמֹכָה בָּאֵלִם, יְיָ?

Who is like You, majestic in (the) holiness,

2. מִי כָּמֹכָה, נֶאְדָּר בַּקֹּדֶשׁ,

Awesome in splendor, doing wonders?

3. נוֹרָא תְהִלֹת, עֹשֵׂה פֶלֶא?

....

Now read the line following מִי כָמֹכָה.

יְיָ יִמְלֹךְ לְעוֹלָם וָעֶד.

Adonai will rule forever and ever.

....

Which three letters in יִמְלֹךְ tell us that "rule" is part of the word's meaning?

Write the three letters. _____ _____ _____

These three letters are called the _____ .

Write the phrase that means "forever and ever." _____

TRUE OR FALSE

Put a ✔ next to each sentence that is true.

_____ In מִי כָמֹכָה we say that there is none greater than God.

_____ מִי כָמֹכָה is read only once a day in the synagogue.

_____ מִי כָמֹכָה was first sung when the Children of Israel crossed the Sea of Reeds.

_____ מִי כָמֹכָה comes from the Book of Genesis in the Torah.

_____ מִי כָמֹכָה is a song of thanks to God.

ROOTS

The word בַּקֹדֶשׁ is built on the root קדשׁ.

The root קדשׁ means "holy."

The root קדשׁ tells us that "holy" is part of the word's meaning.

Circle the three root letters in this word.

בַּקֹדֶשׁ

Write the root. _____ _____ _____

What does the root mean? _____

Circle the three root letters in each of these words. Read the words aloud.

קָדְשֵׁנוּ   הַקָּדוֹשׁ   וְתִתְקַדֵּשׁ   קָדְשׁוֹ   קָדוֹשׁ

BACK TO THE SOURCES

This is a page from the Book of Exodus. It is the song the Children of Israel sang after they crossed the Sea of Reeds. The Torah says that the waters of the Sea of Reeds formed a wall to the right and to the left of the Children of Israel as they crossed on dry land. Do you think the text resembles a wall of bricks?

Can you find and read the first three lines of מִי כָמֹכָה?

Can you find and read the line following מִי כָמֹכָה?

---

9 אָמַר

אוֹיֵב אֶרְדֹּף אַשִּׂיג אֲחַלֵּק שָׁלָל תִּמְלָאֵמוֹ

י נַפְשִׁי אָרִיק חַרְבִּי תּוֹרִישֵׁמוֹ יָדִי: נָשַׁפְתָּ

בְרוּחֲךָ כִּסָּמוֹ יָם צָלֲלוּ כַּעוֹפֶרֶת בְּמַיִם

11 מִי אַדִּירִים: מִי־כָמֹכָה בָּאֵלִם יְהֹוָה

כָּמֹכָה נֶאְדָּר בַּקֹּדֶשׁ נוֹרָא תְהִלֹּת עֹשֵׂה־

12 13 נָחִיתָ פֶלֶא: נָטִיתָ יְמִינְךָ תִּבְלָעֵמוֹ אָרֶץ:

בְחַסְדְּךָ עַם־זוּ גָּאָלְתָּ נֵהַלְתָּ בְעָזְּךָ אֶל־נְוֵה

14 חִיל קָדְשֶׁךָ: שָׁמְעוּ עַמִּים יִרְגָּזוּן

טו אָחַז יֹשְׁבֵי פְּלָשֶׁת: אָז נִבְהֲלוּ אַלּוּפֵי

נָמֹגוּ אֱדוֹם אֵילֵי מוֹאָב יֹאחֲזֵמוֹ רָעַד

16 כֹּל יֹשְׁבֵי כְנָעַן: תִּפֹּל עֲלֵיהֶם אֵימָתָה

עַד־ וָפַחַד בִּגְדֹל זְרוֹעֲךָ יִדְּמוּ כָּאָבֶן

יַעֲבֹר עַמְּךָ יְהֹוָה עַד־יַעֲבֹר עַם־זוּ

17 מָכוֹן קָנִיתָ: תְּבִאֵמוֹ וְתִטָּעֵמוֹ בְּהַר נַחֲלָתְךָ

לְשִׁבְתְּךָ פָּעַלְתָּ יְהֹוָה מִקְּדָשׁ אֲדֹנָי כּוֹנֲנוּ

18 19 יָדֶיךָ: יְהֹוָה ׀ יִמְלֹךְ לְעֹלָם וָעֶד:

Prayer Building Blocks

בַּקֹּדֶשׁ "in (the) holiness"

בַּקֹּדֶשׁ means "in (the) holiness."

בַּקֹּדֶשׁ is made up of two parts:

בַּ means "in the."

קֹדֶשׁ means "holiness."

Circle the word part that means "in the." בַּקֹּדֶשׁ

Write the word part that means "in the." _____

בָּאֵלִם "among the gods"

בָּאֵלִם means "among the gods."

בָּאֵלִם is made up of two parts:

בָּ means "among the" or "in the."

אֵלִם means "gods"—the many false gods that people worshipped.

Circle the part of the word that means "among the" or "in the." בָּאֵלִם

Write the word part that means "among the" or "in the." _____

Note: בְּ *means "in."*

READING PRACTICE

Practice reading these words.

Circle the word parts that mean "in" or "in the."

1. בַּקֹּדֶשׁ   בָּאֵלִם   בְּחֶסֶד   בִּקְדֻשָׁתוֹ   בְּכָל

2. בַּשָּׁמַיִם   בְּחֵן   בַּיּוֹם   בַּיָּמִים   בִּזְמַן

49

Practice reading the lines below.

1. מִי־כָמֹכָה בָּאֵלִם, יְיָ?

2. מִי כָּמֹכָה, נֶאְדָּר בַּקֹּדֶשׁ,

3. נוֹרָא תְהִלֹּת, עֹשֵׂה פֶלֶא?

4. מִי כָמוֹךָ, בַּעַל גְּבוּרוֹת, וּמִי דוֹמֶה לָּךְ?

5. אֵין כָּמוֹךָ חַנּוּן וְרַחוּם, יְיָ אֱלֹהֵינוּ.

6. אֵין כָּמוֹךָ, אֵל, אֶרֶךְ אַפַּיִם וְרַב חֶסֶד וֶאֱמֶת.

7. רַחֵם עָלֵינוּ וְעַל כָּל מַעֲשֶׂיךָ, כִּי אֵין כָּמוֹךָ, יְיָ אֱלֹהֵינוּ.

8. תְּהִלַּת יְיָ יְדַבֶּר פִּי, וִיבָרֵךְ כָּל בָּשָׂר שֵׁם קָדְשׁוֹ.

9. מִי יַעֲלֶה בְהַר יְיָ, וּמִי יָקוּם בִּמְקוֹם קָדְשׁוֹ?

10. וְאַתָּה קָדוֹשׁ, יוֹשֵׁב תְּהִלּוֹת יִשְׂרָאֵל.

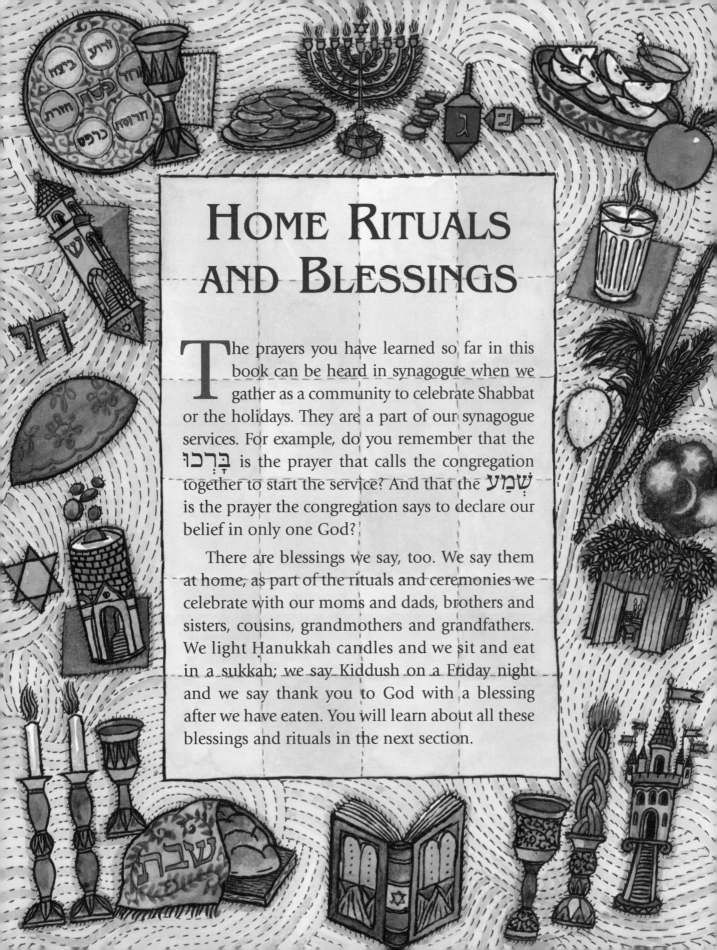

HOME RITUALS AND BLESSINGS

The prayers you have learned so far in this book can be heard in synagogue when we gather as a community to celebrate Shabbat or the holidays. They are a part of our synagogue services. For example, do you remember that the בָּרְכוּ is the prayer that calls the congregation together to start the service? And that the שְׁמַע is the prayer the congregation says to declare our belief in only one God?

There are blessings we say, too. We say them at home, as part of the rituals and ceremonies we celebrate with our moms and dads, brothers and sisters, cousins, grandmothers and grandfathers. We light Hanukkah candles and we sit and eat in a sukkah; we say Kiddush on a Friday night and we say thank you to God with a blessing after we have eaten. You will learn about all these blessings and rituals in the next section.

בְּרָכוֹת

There are lots of people we thank for many things, every day. You may thank your dad for making lunch, your aunt for driving you to baseball practice, or your best friend for a birthday present. Just as we say thanks with words, a hug, a note or an e-mail, we say thank you for God's gifts with prayers called בְּרָכוֹת. There are different kinds of בְּרָכוֹת—blessings—for the different things we are grateful for, like waking up, eating or even seeing something beautiful. Most בְּרָכוֹת begin with the same six words.

Practice reading the six words.

בָּרוּךְ אַתָּה, יְיָ אֱלֹהֵינוּ, מֶלֶךְ הָעוֹלָם...

Praised are You, Adonai our God, Ruler of the world . . .

PRAYER DICTIONARY

בָּרוּךְ
praised, blessed

אַתָּה
you

יְיָ
Adonai

אֱלֹהֵינוּ
our God

מֶלֶךְ
ruler

הָעוֹלָם
the world

SEARCH AND CIRCLE

Circle the Hebrew word that means the same as the English.

Adonai	שֵׁם	יְיָ	אַתָּה
ruler	מֶלֶךְ	כְּבוֹד	יִשְׂרָאֵל
the world	נֶאְדָּר	הָעוֹלָם	כָּמְכָה
our God	בָּאֵלִם	מַלְכוּתוֹ	אֱלֹהֵינוּ
praised	שְׁמַע	בַּקֹּדֶשׁ	בָּרוּךְ
you	אַתָּה	מִי	אֶחָד

FIND THE WORDS

How many words in the Prayer Dictionary refer to God? _____

Write them here.

_____

_____

53

BEGINNINGS AND ENDINGS

For each blessing, underline the six words that usually begin a בְּרָכָה—a blessing.

1. בָּרוּךְ אַתָּה, יְיָ אֱלֹהֵינוּ, מֶלֶךְ הָעוֹלָם, בּוֹרֵא פְּרִי הַגָּפֶן.

2. בָּרוּךְ אַתָּה, יְיָ אֱלֹהֵינוּ, מֶלֶךְ הָעוֹלָם, הַמּוֹצִיא לֶחֶם מִן הָאָרֶץ.

3. בָּרוּךְ אַתָּה, יְיָ אֱלֹהֵינוּ, מֶלֶךְ הָעוֹלָם, בּוֹרֵא מִינֵי מְזוֹנוֹת.

Now *write* the words that usually begin a בְּרָכָה.

_____

The first six words of a blessing are usually the same,
but the ending changes according to what you are thanking God for.

Circle the endings of the three blessings above.

Which of these blessings is said over ḥallah? Write the number: _____

DID YOU KNOW?

When we finish saying a blessing, the people around us respond with "Amen."

What does "Amen" mean?

Amen comes from the root אמן which means "believe" or "have faith." (אֱמוּנָה, "faith," comes from the same root.) When we say Amen, we are showing that we agree with the person who is saying the blessing. We are expressing our faith in God.

Prayer Building Blocks

בָּרוּךְ "blessed" or "praised"

בָּרוּךְ shares a common root with the Hebrew word בֶּרֶךְ, "knee."

בָּרוּךְ reminds us that praising or blessing Adonai is like kneeling in front of a ruler. When we say a בְּרָכָה it is as if we are kneeling before Adonai, our Ruler.

בָּרוּךְ is built on the root _____ _____ _____.

בֶּרֶךְ is built on the root _____ _____ _____.

בְּרָכָה is built on the root _____ _____ _____.

This root means "blessed" or "praised."

Write the root letters. _____ _____ _____

What does this root mean? _____

אַתָּה "you"

When we say a blessing we speak directly to God. We use the Hebrew word אַתָּה to address God. We talk to God as a friend who is near us.

The Hebrew word for "you" is _____.

Fill in the missing word below.

בָּרוּךְ _____ ,יְיָ אֱלֹהֵינוּ ,מֶלֶךְ הָעוֹלָם

מֶלֶךְ "ruler"

In a בְּרָכָה we call God "You," just as we would a friend. But a moment later we address God as "Ruler." We have many kinds of relationships with God.

God is our friend and our sovereign.

The word מֶלֶךְ literally means "king." Because God is neither male nor female, we translate מֶלֶךְ as "ruler."

מֶלֶךְ is built on the root _____ _____ _____.

This root means _____.

Circle the three root letters in each of the words below.

מַלְכִי   הַמְּלָכִים   מֶלֶךְ   מַלְכוּתְךָ

(Hint: כך *are family letters.)*

הָעוֹלָם "the world" "the universe"

God is not just Ruler of the Jewish people. God is Ruler of the whole world.

הָעוֹלָם   means "the world" or "the universe."

עוֹלָם   means "world" or "universe."

הָ   means "the."

Circle the part of each Hebrew word which means "the" in each example below.

הָאֲדָמָה   הָעֵץ   הַגֶּפֶן   הָאָרֶץ   הָעוֹלָם

What does הָ or הַ mean? _____

BLESSING MATCH

Draw a line between the blessing and its matching picture.

1.
בָּרוּךְ אַתָּה, יְיָ אֱלֹהֵינוּ,
מֶלֶךְ הָעוֹלָם,
בּוֹרֵא פְּרִי הַגָּפֶן.

Praised are You, Adonai our God,
Ruler of the world,
who creates the fruit of the vine.

2.
בָּרוּךְ אַתָּה, יְיָ אֱלֹהֵינוּ,
מֶלֶךְ הָעוֹלָם,
הַמּוֹצִיא לֶחֶם מִן הָאָרֶץ.

Praised are You, Adonai our God,
Ruler of the world,
who brings forth bread from the earth.

3.
בָּרוּךְ אַתָּה, יְיָ אֱלֹהֵינוּ,
מֶלֶךְ הָעוֹלָם,
בּוֹרֵא פְּרִי הָאֲדָמָה.

Praised are You, Adonai our God,
Ruler of the world,
who creates the fruit of the earth (vegetables).

4.
בָּרוּךְ אַתָּה, יְיָ אֱלֹהֵינוּ,
מֶלֶךְ הָעוֹלָם,
בּוֹרֵא מִינֵי מְזוֹנוֹת.

Praised are You, Adonai our God,
Ruler of the world,
who creates baked goods.

DID YOU KNOW?

The Talmud teaches that Jews should say at least 100 בְּרָכוֹת each day!

One hundred blessings in a single day?

In fact, if you added up all the בְּרָכוֹת in the three daily synagogue services plus some of the extra blessings said during the day, you would easily reach 100.

Can you think of 100 things for which you are grateful?

(Hints: a loving family, a nice home, good health—what else?)

An Ethical Echo

Saying a בְּרָכָה makes us stop and appreciate the world around us. We thank God and show that we do not take God's creations for granted. We are the caretakers of God's world. We show our respect for God by treating God's world—our earth—with respect. In the Torah, this commandment is called *Bal Tashhit*—בַּל תַּשְׁחִית—Preserving the Earth.

Think About This!

Can you think of ways to treat the earth with respect?

בִּרְכַּת הַמָּזוֹן

How do you feel after you've finished a delicious dinner that your mom or dad made? Probably full and happy—and pleased that they took the time to cook for you. Just as you thank your mom or dad after dinner for preparing such a great meal, we thank God after our meal by saying בִּרְכַּת הַמָּזוֹן.

בִּרְכַּת הַמָּזוֹן thanks God for more than providing us with the food we've just eaten. It also thanks God for the Land of Israel and the Torah, and it praises God's goodness and kindness. We enjoy feeling full—filled with food and filled with God's gifts—and we thank God for allowing us to enjoy them all.

Practice reading this section of בִּרְכַּת הַמָּזוֹן.

1. בָּרוּךְ אַתָּה, יְיָ אֱלֹהֵינוּ, מֶלֶךְ הָעוֹלָם,

2. הַזָּן אֶת הָעוֹלָם כֻּלּוֹ בְּטוּבוֹ,

3. בְּחֵן בְּחֶסֶד וּבְרַחֲמִים.

4. הוּא נוֹתֵן לֶחֶם לְכָל בָּשָׂר, כִּי לְעוֹלָם חַסְדּוֹ.

5. וּבְטוּבוֹ הַגָּדוֹל תָּמִיד לֹא חָסַר לָנוּ,

6. וְאַל יֶחְסַר לָנוּ מָזוֹן לְעוֹלָם וָעֶד.

7. בַּעֲבוּר שְׁמוֹ הַגָּדוֹל כִּי הוּא אֵל זָן וּמְפַרְנֵס לַכֹּל,

8. וּמֵטִיב לַכֹּל, וּמֵכִין מָזוֹן לְכָל בְּרִיּוֹתָיו אֲשֶׁר בָּרָא.

9. בָּרוּךְ אַתָּה יְיָ, הַזָּן אֶת הַכֹּל.

DID YOU KNOW?

The full בִּרְכַּת הַמָּזוֹן is said only after a meal at which bread has been consumed. You can see how important bread really is.

בִּרְכוֹת שֶׁל מִצְוָה

We also say a בְּרָכָה when we carry out certain commandments from God. All of God's commandments are known as mitzvot, and particular ones—like studying Torah, blowing the shofar on the High Holy Days, or sitting and eating in a sukkah on Sukkot—require us to say a blessing when we perform them. Every בְּרָכָה שֶׁל מִצְוָה begins with the same ten words.

Practice reading these words.

1. בָּרוּךְ אַתָּה, יְיָ אֱלֹהֵינוּ, מֶלֶךְ הָעוֹלָם,

2. אֲשֶׁר קִדְּשָׁנוּ בְּמִצְוֹתָיו וְצִוָּנוּ...

Praised are You, Adonai our God, Ruler of the world,
who makes us holy with God's commandments and commands us . . .

Think About This!

Because so many of God's commandments—mitzvot—require us to be good and decent, many people consider a mitzvah to be a "good deed." You perform mitzvot every day without even realizing it—like visiting your best friend when she's home with a cold, trying not to gossip about kids at school, or even feeding your puppy before you eat your own dinner! What other kinds of "good deed" mitzvot do you do?

אֲשֶׁר
who

קִדְּשָׁנוּ
makes us holy

בְּמִצְוֹתָיו
with God's
commandments

וְצִוָּנוּ
and commands us

WORD MATCH

Match the English word to its Hebrew meaning.

A. with God's commandments   אֲשֶׁר ( )

B. who   קִדְּשָׁנוּ ( )

C. and commands us   בְּמִצְוֹתָיו ( )

D. makes us holy   וְצִוָּנוּ ( )

DID YOU NOTICE?

There are four words that help us recognize a
בְּרָכָה שֶׁל מִצְוָה. The words are:

אֲשֶׁר קִדְּשָׁנוּ בְּמִצְוֹתָיו וְצִוָּנוּ

Fill in the four words that help us recognize a
בְּרָכָה שֶׁל מִצְוָה.

בָּרוּךְ אַתָּה, יְיָ אֱלֹהֵינוּ, מֶלֶךְ הָעוֹלָם

_____ _____ _____ _____

Prayer Building Blocks

קִדְּשָׁנוּ "makes us holy"

קִדְּשָׁנוּ   means "makes us holy."

קִדְּשָׁנוּ   is made up of two parts:

קִדְּשָׁ   means "makes holy."

נוּ   means "us" or "our."

Add the ending that means "us" to complete this word:

קִדְּשָׁ _____

makes us holy

קִדְּשָׁנוּ is built on the root _____ _____ _____.

This root means _____.

בְּמִצְוֹתָיו "with God's commandments"

בְּמִצְוֹתָיו   means "with God's commandments."

בְּמִצְוֹתָיו   is made up of three parts:

בְּ   at the beginning of a word means "with" or "in."

מִצְוֹת   means "commandments."

יו   at the end of a word means "his."

As God is neither male nor female, we translate the word בְּמִצְוֹתָיו as "with God's commandments."

Write the part of the Hebrew word that means "with." _____

Circle the Hebrew word below that means "commandments."

מַצָּה   מִצְוָה   מִצְוֹת

וְצִוָּנוּ "and commands us"

וְצִוָּנוּ means "and commands us."

וְצִוָּנוּ is made up of three parts:

וְ means "and."

צִוָּ means "commands."

נוּ means "us."

Write the Hebrew word that means "and commands us." _____

The letters וֹ and צ appear in both of the following words:

בְּמִצְוֹתָיו   וְצִוָּנוּ

with God's commandments   and commands us

Draw a circle around the letters וֹ and צ in the middle of the two words above.

The letters וֹ and צ let us know that "command" is part of a word's meaning.

LOOK ALIKES

Sometimes the letter *vav* looks like this: וֹ

It looks like the vowel sound "oh": טוֹ בוֹ קוֹ.

However, וֹ has the sound "vo" if it follows a letter that already has a vowel, as in עֲוֹ and צְוֹ.

Read each sound aloud.

עֲוֹ   עוֹ   צְוֹ   עֲוֹ

צְוֹ   עוֹ   צוֹ   צְוֹ

Practice reading the following words.

רְצוֹנְךָ	מִצְוָה	עֶוֹנִי	רָצָה	מִצְוֹת	.1
עֲוֹנַתִי	לִרְצוֹן	מִצְוֹתַי	צוֹדֵק	רָצוֹן	.2
בְּמִצְוֹתָיו	אַרְצוֹת	מִצְרַיִם	בְּמִצְוֹת	וְצִוָּנוּ	.3
מְצוֹרָע	צוֹרֶךְ	צוֹפִיָּה	מַצוֹת	עָוֹן	.4
מִצִּיוֹן	צִוָּה	עוֹנָה	מִצְוַת	בְּמִצְוֹתַי	.5

FLUENT READING

Practice reading the lines below.

1. בָּרוּךְ אַתָּה, יְיָ אֱלֹהֵינוּ, מֶלֶךְ הָעוֹלָם,
אֲשֶׁר קִדְּשָׁנוּ בְּמִצְוֹתָיו וְצִוָּנוּ לְהָנִיחַ תְּפִלִּין.

2. בָּרוּךְ אַתָּה, יְיָ אֱלֹהֵינוּ, מֶלֶךְ הָעוֹלָם,
אֲשֶׁר קִדְּשָׁנוּ בְּמִצְוֹתָיו וְצִוָּנוּ עַל נְטִילַת לוּלָב.

3. בָּרוּךְ אַתָּה, יְיָ אֱלֹהֵינוּ, מֶלֶךְ הָעוֹלָם,
אֲשֶׁר קִדְּשָׁנוּ בְּמִצְוֹתָיו וְצִוָּנוּ עַל מִצְוַת תְּפִלִּין.

4. בָּרוּךְ אַתָּה, יְיָ אֱלֹהֵינוּ, מֶלֶךְ הָעוֹלָם,
אֲשֶׁר בִּדְבָרוֹ מַעֲרִיב עֲרָבִים.

5. בָּרוּךְ אַתָּה, יְיָ אֱלֹהֵינוּ, מֶלֶךְ הָעוֹלָם,
אֲשֶׁר נָתַן לָנוּ תּוֹרַת אֱמֶת.

6. בָּרוּךְ אַתָּה, יְיָ אֱלֹהֵינוּ, מֶלֶךְ הָעוֹלָם,
אֲשֶׁר קִדְּשָׁנוּ בְּמִצְוֹתָיו וְצִוָּנוּ לַעֲסוֹק בְּדִבְרֵי תוֹרָה.

בִּרְכוֹת שֶׁל שַׁבָּת

Shabbat is a time of peace, a time for family. There are special בְּרָכוֹת with which we welcome Shabbat into our homes. When we say בְּרָכוֹת over the candles, wine, and ḥallah, we are thanking God for creating the Shabbat and allowing us to celebrate it.

Practice reading the בְּרָכוֹת **aloud.**

1. בָּרוּךְ אַתָּה, יְיָ אֱלֹהֵינוּ, מֶלֶךְ הָעוֹלָם, אֲשֶׁר קִדְּשָׁנוּ בְּמִצְוֹתָיו וְצִוָּנוּ לְהַדְלִיק נֵר שֶׁל שַׁבָּת.

Praised are You, Adonai our God, Ruler of the world, who makes us holy with commandments and commands us to light the Sabbath light (candles).

2. בָּרוּךְ אַתָּה, יְיָ אֱלֹהֵינוּ, מֶלֶךְ הָעוֹלָם, בּוֹרֵא פְּרִי הַגָּפֶן.

Praised are You, Adonai our God, Ruler of the world, who creates the fruit of the vine.

3. בָּרוּךְ אַתָּה, יְיָ אֱלֹהֵינוּ, מֶלֶךְ הָעוֹלָם, הַמּוֹצִיא לֶחֶם מִן הָאָרֶץ.

Praised are You, Adonai our God, Ruler of the world, who brings forth bread from the earth.

NAME THE SHABBAT OBJECT

Complete each sentence by writing the English word or drawing a picture.

Blessing #1 is said over the	Blessing #2 is said over the	Blessing #3 is said over the

LIGHTING THE CANDLES

The first Shabbat בְּרָכָה we say is over the candles. Saying the בְּרָכָה helps us usher in Shabbat with brightness and joy. Once the candles have been lit at sunset and the בְּרָכָה has been said, Shabbat has begun.

Practice reading the בְּרָכָה.

בָּרוּךְ אַתָּה, יְיָ אֱלֹהֵינוּ, מֶלֶךְ הָעוֹלָם, אֲשֶׁר
קִדְּשָׁנוּ בְּמִצְוֹתָיו וְצִוָּנוּ לְהַדְלִיק נֵר שֶׁל שַׁבָּת.

Praised are You, Adonai our God, Ruler of the world, who makes us holy with commandments and commands us to light the Sabbath light (candles).

MATCH GAME

Connect the Hebrew word to its English meaning.

to light	בָּרוּךְ
light, candle	שַׁבָּת
Shabbat	נֵר
praised	לְהַדְלִיק

UNSCRAMBLE THE PRAYER

Write the ending of the candle blessing in the correct order.

בָּרוּךְ אַתָּה, יְיָ אֱלֹהֵינוּ, מֶלֶךְ הָעוֹלָם, אֲשֶׁר קִדְּשָׁנוּ
בְּמִצְוֹתָיו וְצִוָּנוּ . . .

שַׁבָּת לְהַדְלִיק שֶׁל נֵר

_____

DID YOU KNOW?

Do you know why we light *two* candles on Shabbat?

The Ten Commandments appear twice in the Torah.

The first time—in the Book of Exodus—Adonai tells us: "*Remember* the Shabbat."

The second time—in the Book of Deuteronomy—Adonai tells us: "*Observe* the Shabbat."

The two candles remind us of both these commandments.

Some people light more than two candles. In some homes candles are lit for every member of the family. There is no limit to the number of candles you can light.

CANDLES AND LIGHT

Candles and light play an important role in Judaism. The Ḥanukkah candles flicker and glow on your window ledge. We light a *yahrzeit* candle to remember the anniversary of a loved one's death. And the Eternal Light always burns above the Holy Ark.

Practice reading each of these blessings recited over candles.

1. בָּרוּךְ אַתָּה, יְיָ אֱלֹהֵינוּ, מֶלֶךְ הָעוֹלָם, אֲשֶׁר קִדְּשָׁנוּ בְּמִצְוֹתָיו וְצִוָּנוּ לְהַדְלִיק נֵר שֶׁל שַׁבָּת.

2. בָּרוּךְ אַתָּה, יְיָ אֱלֹהֵינוּ, מֶלֶךְ הָעוֹלָם, אֲשֶׁר קִדְּשָׁנוּ בְּמִצְוֹתָיו וְצִוָּנוּ לְהַדְלִיק נֵר שֶׁל יוֹם טוֹב.

3. בָּרוּךְ אַתָּה, יְיָ אֱלֹהֵינוּ, מֶלֶךְ הָעוֹלָם, אֲשֶׁר קִדְּשָׁנוּ בְּמִצְוֹתָיו וְצִוָּנוּ לְהַדְלִיק נֵר שֶׁל שַׁבָּת וְשֶׁל יוֹם טוֹב.

4. בָּרוּךְ אַתָּה, יְיָ אֱלֹהֵינוּ, מֶלֶךְ הָעוֹלָם, אֲשֶׁר קִדְּשָׁנוּ בְּמִצְוֹתָיו וְצִוָּנוּ לְהַדְלִיק נֵר שֶׁל חֲנֻכָּה.

5. בָּרוּךְ אַתָּה, יְיָ אֱלֹהֵינוּ, מֶלֶךְ הָעוֹלָם, בּוֹרֵא מְאוֹרֵי הָאֵשׁ.

Do you recognize the blessing over the Ḥanukkah candles?

Write its number here. _____

FOOD FOR THOUGHT

A blessing is usually said *before* the action takes place. For example, when we eat an apple, first we say the בְּרָכָה (...בּוֹרֵא פְּרִי הָעֵץ), and then we take the first bite.

But in the case of the Shabbat candles, we light the candles *first* and say the blessing *afterward*.

Why?

Once we say the blessing, Shabbat begins. Many people will not light a match on Shabbat. Therefore, first we light the match (and the candles), and then we say the blessing.

בּוֹרֵא

who creates

פְּרִי

(the) fruit (of)

הַגָּפֶן

the vine

BLESSING FOR THE WINE

The Kiddush is the בְּרָכָה we say over wine. קִדּוּשׁ—Kiddush—comes from the word that means "making holy." This בְּרָכָה helps us sanctify Shabbat and make it holy. Traditionally, before the Shabbat קִדּוּשׁ is recited, we fill the wineglass to overflowing to thank God for our abundance of blessings. In the Shabbat קִדּוּשׁ we express our joy as we remember two occasions—when God created the universe and when we were freed from slavery in Egypt.

Complete the following activities for the blessing over the wine.

בָּרוּךְ אַתָּה, יְיָ אֱלֹהֵינוּ, מֶלֶךְ הָעוֹלָם,
בּוֹרֵא פְּרִי הַגָּפֶן.

Praised are You, Adonai our God, Ruler of the world, who creates the fruit of the vine.

1. Circle the word that means "fruit."

2. Draw a box around the Hebrew word that means "who creates."

3. Underline the word for "praised."

4. Write the English meaning of מֶלֶךְ. _____

5. Put a star over the word for "the vine."

6. Write the part of הָעוֹלָם that means "the." _____

7. Write the part of הַגָּפֶן that means "the." _____

8. What is another English word for "the fruit of the vine"?

_____

71

BLESSING FOR THE BREAD

On Shabbat, we also say הַמּוֹצִיא—the בְּרָכָה for bread—over the specially braided ḥallah to praise and thank God for giving us food to eat. Remember that there are בְּרָכוֹת we can say before eating any kind of food—breakfast cereal, a cheese sandwich, or even your family's special chicken dish!

Practice reading הַמּוֹצִיא.

1. בָּרוּךְ אַתָּה, יְיָ אֱלֹהֵינוּ, מֶלֶךְ הָעוֹלָם,

2. הַמּוֹצִיא לֶחֶם מִן הָאָרֶץ.

Praised are You, Adonai our God, Ruler of the world,
who brings forth bread from the earth.

DID YOU KNOW?

Bread is the symbol of food in Jewish life.

In the Bible there are many examples of guests being offered bread to eat. Abraham and Sarah, who are famous for their hospitality, immediately served bread to make their guests feel welcome.

In fact, bread is so important that one blessing said at the beginning of a meal—הַמּוֹצִיא—covers all the food to be eaten during that meal.

הַמוֹצִיא

who brings forth

לֶחֶם

bread

מִן

from

הָאָרֶץ

the earth

WORD MATCH

Match the English word to its Hebrew meaning.

A. who brings forth   מִן ( )

B. the earth   הָאָרֶץ ( )

C. bread   לֶחֶם ( )

D. from   הַמוֹצִיא ( )

UNSCRAMBLE THE PRAYER

Write the ending of the בְּרָכָה in the correct order.

בָּרוּךְ אַתָּה, יְיָ אֱלֹהֵינוּ, מֶלֶךְ הָעוֹלָם . . .

מִן   הַמוֹצִיא   הָאָרֶץ   לֶחֶם

_____

An Ethical Echo

In the Book of Deuteronomy there is a passage that says "Befriend strangers, for you were strangers in the Land of Egypt." What better way is there to welcome strangers than to open your home to them? The mitzvah of *Hospitality* (הַכְנָסַת אוֹרְחִים—*Hachnasat Orḥim*) is made greater when you offer your guests food and drink.

Think About This!

A new student joins your class in the middle of the school year. What can you do to befriend this stranger?

THE HOLIDAY CONNECTION

As we begin to tell the Passover story at our seder, we uncover a plate of matzah and lift it up for all at the table to see. As we recall that our ancestors ate this "bread of affliction" when they were slaves in Egypt, we announce: "Let all who are hungry come and eat."

Think About This!

Why is the mitzvah of *Feeding the Hungry* (מַאֲכִיל רְעֵבִים—*Ma'achil Re'evim*) so closely linked to our lives in Egypt? How can we fulfill this mitzvah?

הַבְדָּלָה

Do you remember how we welcome Shabbat into our homes? We say בְּרָכוֹת over candles, wine, and ḥallah. There's also a special way that we say goodbye to Shabbat—with the Havdalah blessings.

הַבְדָּלָה means "separation." When we say the Havdalah blessings over wine, sweet spices, and a special braided candle, we are separating the uniqueness of Shabbat from the rest of the week. These blessings thank God for allowing us to celebrate Shabbat and ask God to help us remember its holiness throughout the next six days.

Imagine how you feel on your birthday. It's a special day, when everyone gives you extra attention with gifts, good wishes, and cake. Even when it's over, you can keep that wonderful feeling with you all year long by looking at photos or watching a video of your birthday party. It's the same with הַבְדָּלָה—the scent of the sweet spices and the bright light of the candle help us keep the Shabbat feeling with us all week long.

Practice reading the blessings over the wine, the spices, and the lit candle.

בָּרוּךְ אַתָּה, יְיָ אֱלֹהֵינוּ, מֶלֶךְ הָעוֹלָם, בּוֹרֵא פְּרִי הַגָּפֶן.

Praised are You, Adonai our God, Ruler of the world, who creates the fruit of the vine.

בָּרוּךְ אַתָּה, יְיָ אֱלֹהֵינוּ, מֶלֶךְ הָעוֹלָם, בּוֹרֵא מִינֵי בְשָׂמִים.

Praised are You, Adonai our God, Ruler of the world, who creates the varieties of spice.

בָּרוּךְ אַתָּה, יְיָ אֱלֹהֵינוּ, מֶלֶךְ הָעוֹלָם, בּוֹרֵא מְאוֹרֵי הָאֵשׁ.

Praised are You, Adonai our God, Ruler of the world, who creates the fiery lights.

Now read the blessing that separates the holy day of Shabbat from the other days of the week.

בָּרוּךְ אַתָּה, יְיָ אֱלֹהֵינוּ, מֶלֶךְ הָעוֹלָם, הַמַּבְדִּיל בֵּין קֹדֶשׁ לְחוֹל, בֵּין אוֹר לְחֹשֶׁךְ, בֵּין יִשְׂרָאֵל לָעַמִּים, בֵּין יוֹם הַשְּׁבִיעִי לְשֵׁשֶׁת יְמֵי הַמַּעֲשֶׂה. בָּרוּךְ אַתָּה יְיָ, הַמַּבְדִּיל בֵּין קֹדֶשׁ לְחוֹל.

Praised are You, Adonai our God, Ruler of the world, who separates the holy from the everyday, light from darkness, Israel from the other nations, the seventh day from the six days of work. Praised are You, Adonai, who separates the holy from the everyday.

Think About This!

Why do you think we need to separate Shabbat from the other days of the week?

FLUENT READING

Practice reading the lines below.

1. וְשַׁבַּת קָדְשׁוֹ בְּאַהֲבָה וּבְרָצוֹן הִנְחִילָנוּ.

2. וְשָׁמְרוּ בְנֵי יִשְׂרָאֵל אֶת הַשַּׁבָּת,
לַעֲשׂוֹת אֶת הַשַּׁבָּת לְדֹרֹתָם.

3. בָּרוּךְ אַתָּה, יְיָ אֱלֹהֵינוּ, מֶלֶךְ הָעוֹלָם,
עֹשֶׂה מַעֲשֵׂה בְרֵאשִׁית.

4. בְּרֵאשִׁית בָּרָא אֱלֹהִים אֵת הַשָּׁמַיִם וְאֵת הָאָרֶץ.

5. אֲדוֹן הַשָּׁלוֹם, מְקַדֵּשׁ הַשַּׁבָּת וּמְבָרֵךְ שְׁבִיעִי.

6. בָּרוּךְ אַתָּה יְיָ, מֶלֶךְ עַל כָּל הָאָרֶץ.

7. מְקַדֵּשׁ יִשְׂרָאֵל וְיוֹם הַזִּכָּרוֹן.

8. זִכָּרוֹן לְמַעֲשֵׂה בְרֵאשִׁית.

9. טוֹבִים מְאוֹרוֹת שֶׁבָּרָא אֱלֹהֵינוּ.

10. בָּרוּךְ אַתָּה, יְיָ אֱלֹהֵינוּ, מֶלֶךְ הָעוֹלָם,
אֲשֶׁר קִדְּשָׁנוּ בְּמִצְוֹתָיו וְצִוָּנוּ לְהַדְלִיק נֵר שֶׁל שַׁבָּת.

בִּרְכוֹת שֶׁל יוֹם טוֹב

Just as there are special בְּרָכוֹת for the things we are grateful for during the week and on Shabbat, there are also special blessings for the Jewish holidays.

From Rosh Hashanah and Yom Kippur, to Sukkot, Simḥat Torah, Ḥanukkah, Purim, Pesaḥ and more, each Jewish holiday—יוֹם טוֹב—has its own wonderful way of saying "thank you" to God.

What are some of the בְּרָכוֹת for the holidays?

ROSH HASHANAH

On Rosh Hashanah, we ask God for a sweet new year by dipping slices of apple into honey while saying the בְּרָכָה for fruit. We also say a בְּרָכָה just before we blow or hear the Shofar.

Practice reading these blessings recited on Rosh Hashanah.
Read the Hebrew name for each of the holiday objects pictured.

1. בָּרוּךְ אַתָּה, יְיָ אֱלֹהֵינוּ, מֶלֶךְ הָעוֹלָם,
   בּוֹרֵא פְּרִי הָעֵץ.

Praised are You, Adonai our God, Ruler of the world,
who creates the fruit of the tree.

דְּבַשׁ

תַּפּוּחַ

2. בָּרוּךְ אַתָּה, יְיָ אֱלֹהֵינוּ, מֶלֶךְ הָעוֹלָם,
   אֲשֶׁר קִדְּשָׁנוּ בְּמִצְוֹתָיו
   וְצִוָּנוּ לִשְׁמֹעַ קוֹל שׁוֹפָר.

Praised are You, Adonai our God, Ruler of the world,
who makes us holy with commandments, and commands us
to hear the sound of the shofar.

שׁוֹפָר

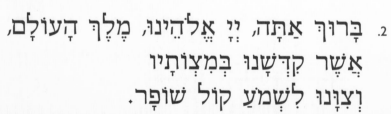

78

פְּרִי
fruit

עֵץ
tree

שׁוֹפָר
shofar

PICTURE MATCH

Connect the Hebrew word to its picture.

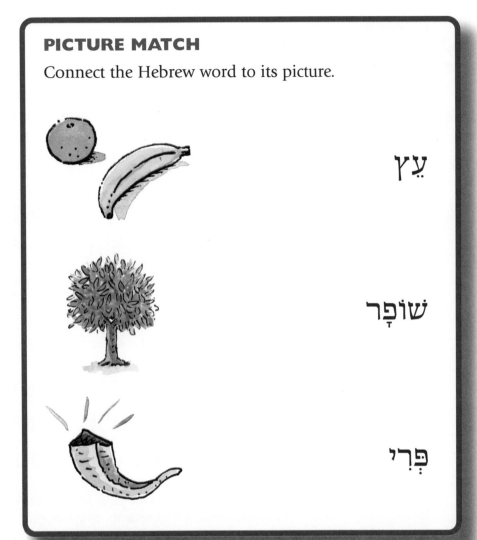

עֵץ

שׁוֹפָר

פְּרִי

SEARCH AND CIRCLE

Circle the Hebrew word that means the same as the English.

tree	אַתָּה	אֶחָד	עֵץ .1
shofar	שׁוֹפָר	יִשְׂרָאֵל	שְׁמַע .2
fruit	מֶלֶךְ	פְּרִי	נֵר .3

בַּסֻכָּה

in the sukkah

לוּלָב

lulav

SUKKOT

On Sukkot, we say a בְּרָכָה when we eat our meals in the sukkah. We remember how our ancestors wandered through the wilderness for forty years before reaching the Land of Israel, living in huts while God provided them with food. When we look up through the branches that form the roof of a sukkah, we can see the same stars our ancestors saw!

Practice reading the בְּרָכָה we say in the sukkah.

בָּרוּךְ אַתָּה, יְיָ אֱלֹהֵינוּ, מֶלֶךְ הָעוֹלָם, אֲשֶׁר קִדְּשָׁנוּ בְּמִצְוֹתָיו וְצִוָּנוּ לֵישֵׁב בַּסֻכָּה.

Praised are You, Adonai our God, Ruler of the world, who makes us holy with commandments and commands us to sit in the sukkah.

Practice reading the בְּרָכָה we say when shaking the lulav.

בָּרוּךְ אַתָּה, יְיָ אֱלֹהֵינוּ, מֶלֶךְ הָעוֹלָם, אֲשֶׁר קִדְּשָׁנוּ בְּמִצְוֹתָיו וְצִוָּנוּ עַל נְטִילַת לוּלָב.

Praised are You, Adonai our God, Ruler of the world, who makes us holy with commandments and commands us to shake the lulav.

חֲנֻכָּה

Ḥanukkah

נִסִּים

miracles

בַּזְּמַן הַזֶּה

at this season,
at this time

שֶׁהֶחֱיָנוּ

who has given
us life

ḤANUKKAH

We say בְּרָכוֹת for eight nights when we light the Ḥanukkah menorah. The Festival of Lights recalls the miracle of the menorah oil burning for eight days instead of just one after Judah Maccabee and his army recaptured the holy Temple in Jerusalem. We celebrate with presents, crispy potato latkes, and games of dreidel!

Practice reading the blessings over the Ḥanukkah candles.

1. בָּרוּךְ אַתָּה, יְיָ אֱלֹהֵינוּ, מֶלֶךְ הָעוֹלָם,
אֲשֶׁר קִדְּשָׁנוּ בְּמִצְוֹתָיו וְצִוָּנוּ
לְהַדְלִיק נֵר שֶׁל חֲנֻכָּה.

Praised are You, Adonai our God, Ruler of the world,
who makes us holy with commandments and commands us
to light the Ḥanukkah candles.

2. בָּרוּךְ אַתָּה, יְיָ אֱלֹהֵינוּ, מֶלֶךְ הָעוֹלָם,
שֶׁעָשָׂה נִסִּים לַאֲבוֹתֵינוּ
בַּיָּמִים הָהֵם בַּזְּמַן הַזֶּה.

Praised are You, Adonai our God, Ruler of the world,
who made miracles for our ancestors long ago, at this season.

On the first night of Ḥanukkah, we also recite a third blessing. In this בְּרָכָה, we thank God for allowing us to celebrate the holiday once again.

3. בָּרוּךְ אַתָּה, יְיָ אֱלֹהֵינוּ, מֶלֶךְ הָעוֹלָם,
שֶׁהֶחֱיָנוּ וְקִיְּמָנוּ וְהִגִּיעָנוּ לַזְּמַן הַזֶּה.

Praised are You, Adonai our God, Ruler of the world,
who has given us life, sustained us, and enabled us to reach this time.

WORD MATCH

Connect the Hebrew to its English meaning.

at this season, at this time   נִסִּים

Hanukkah   שֶׁהֶחֱיָנוּ

miracles   חֲנֻכָּה

who has given us life   בַּזְּמָן הַזֶּה

HOLIDAY DRAWINGS

Read the names of the holidays.
What objects do *you* use to celebrate each one?
Draw or list your favorite holiday objects.

_____ רֹאשׁ הַשָּׁנָה

_____ סֻכּוֹת

_____ שִׂמְחַת תּוֹרָה

_____ חֲנֻכָּה

_____ פּוּרִים

_____ פֶּסַח

An Ethical Echo

Judah Maccabee led a revolt for religious freedom. But religious freedom isn't the only kind of freedom (חֵרוּת) people require to live full, happy lives. What other kinds of freedom do people need?

Think About This!

Can you think of other times when Jews were *not* free? Can you think of other people from the Bible who risked their lives so that the Jewish people could live freely?

82

הָאֲדָמָה

the earth

אֲכִילַת

eating (of)

מַצָּה

matzah

מָרוֹר

maror,
bitter herbs

PESAH

On פֶּסַח we say a blessing over מַצָּה while remembering how God freed us from slavery in Egypt. Because the Jews had to flee in a hurry, there was no time for them to wait for their bread dough to rise. For that reason, we also eat "unrisen" bread—מַצָּה—on פֶּסַח (plus many other delicious foods such as matzah balls and potato kugel!).

Practice reading the blessings we say during the Passover seder.

Drinking the Wine

בָּרוּךְ אַתָּה, יְיָ אֱלֹהֵינוּ, מֶלֶךְ הָעוֹלָם,
בּוֹרֵא פְּרִי הַגָּפֶן.

Praised are You, Adonai our God, Ruler of the world,
who creates the fruit of the vine.

Eating a Green Vegetable

בָּרוּךְ אַתָּה, יְיָ אֱלֹהֵינוּ, מֶלֶךְ הָעוֹלָם,
בּוֹרֵא פְּרִי הָאֲדָמָה.

Praised are You, Adonai our God, Ruler of the world,
who creates the fruit of the earth.

Eating the Matzah

בָּרוּךְ אַתָּה, יְיָ אֱלֹהֵינוּ, מֶלֶךְ הָעוֹלָם,
הַמּוֹצִיא לֶחֶם מִן הָאָרֶץ.

Praised are You, Adonai our God, Ruler of the world,
who brings forth bread from the earth.

בָּרוּךְ אַתָּה, יְיָ אֱלֹהֵינוּ, מֶלֶךְ הָעוֹלָם, אֲשֶׁר
קִדְּשָׁנוּ בְּמִצְוֹתָיו וְצִוָּנוּ עַל אֲכִילַת מַצָּה.

Praised are You, Adonai our God, Ruler of the world, who makes
us holy with commandments, and commands us to eat matzah.

Eating Bitter Herbs

בָּרוּךְ אַתָּה, יְיָ אֱלֹהֵינוּ, מֶלֶךְ הָעוֹלָם, אֲשֶׁר
קִדְּשָׁנוּ בְּמִצְוֹתָיו וְצִוָּנוּ עַל אֲכִילַת מָרוֹר.

Praised are You, Adonai our God, Ruler of the world, who makes
us holy with commandments, and commands us to eat bitter herbs.

PICTURE MATCH

Connect the Hebrew word to its picture.

אֲכִילַת

הָאֲדָמָה

מָרוֹר

מַצָּה

FILL IN THE BLANK

Write the missing word in each blessing ending.

(Hint: It's the same word!)

1. עַל _____ מַצָּה.

2. עַל _____ מָרוֹר.

Do you know what matzah symbolizes? Maror?

FLUENT READING

Practice reading these holiday blessings. Do you know when we say each one?

1. בָּרוּךְ אַתָּה, יְיָ אֱלֹהֵינוּ, מֶלֶךְ הָעוֹלָם,
שֶׁהֶחֱיָנוּ וְקִיְּמָנוּ וְהִגִּיעָנוּ לַזְּמַן הַזֶּה.

2. בָּרוּךְ אַתָּה, יְיָ אֱלֹהֵינוּ, מֶלֶךְ הָעוֹלָם,
אֲשֶׁר קִדְּשָׁנוּ בְּמִצְוֹתָיו וְצִוָּנוּ לְהַדְלִיק נֵר שֶׁל יוֹם טוֹב.

3. בָּרוּךְ אַתָּה, יְיָ אֱלֹהֵינוּ, מֶלֶךְ הָעוֹלָם,
אֲשֶׁר קִדְּשָׁנוּ בְּמִצְוֹתָיו וְצִוָּנוּ עַל מִקְרָא מְגִלָּה.

4. בָּרוּךְ אַתָּה, יְיָ אֱלֹהֵינוּ, מֶלֶךְ הָעוֹלָם,
אֲשֶׁר קִדְּשָׁנוּ בְּמִצְוֹתָיו וְצִוָּנוּ עַל אֲכִילַת מַצָּה.

5. בָּרוּךְ אַתָּה, יְיָ אֱלֹהֵינוּ, מֶלֶךְ הָעוֹלָם,
בּוֹרֵא פְּרִי הָעֵץ.

6. בָּרוּךְ אַתָּה, יְיָ אֱלֹהֵינוּ, מֶלֶךְ הָעוֹלָם,
אֲשֶׁר קִדְּשָׁנוּ בְּמִצְוֹתָיו וְצִוָּנוּ לְהַדְלִיק נֵר שֶׁל חֲנֻכָּה.

7. בָּרוּךְ אַתָּה, יְיָ אֱלֹהֵינוּ, מֶלֶךְ הָעוֹלָם,
אֲשֶׁר קִדְּשָׁנוּ בְּמִצְוֹתָיו וְצִוָּנוּ עַל אֲכִילַת מָרוֹר.

8. בָּרוּךְ אַתָּה, יְיָ אֱלֹהֵינוּ, מֶלֶךְ הָעוֹלָם,
אֲשֶׁר קִדְּשָׁנוּ בְּמִצְוֹתָיו וְצִוָּנוּ עַל נְטִילַת לוּלָב.

קִדוּשׁ

Do you remember that the קִדוּשׁ is one of the בְּרָכוֹת we say to welcome and sanctify Shabbat? We also say it on many holidays, including Rosh Hashanah, Sukkot, and Pesaḥ. The קִדוּשׁ separates these occasions from the everyday and helps us to make them holy.

The קִדוּשׁ begins with the blessing over the wine, thanking God for creating the fruit of the vine—the grapes from which we make wine.

The קִדוּשׁ for Shabbat reminds us that we were chosen by God with love to observe Shabbat and to carry out God's commandments.

The קִדוּשׁ begins with a בְּרָכָה you have already learned.

בָּרוּךְ אַתָּה, יְיָ אֱלֹהֵינוּ, מֶלֶךְ הָעוֹלָם, בּוֹרֵא פְּרִי הַגָּפֶן.

Can you say this בְּרָכָה by heart?

Practice reading the קִדוּשׁ for Shabbat aloud.

1. בָּרוּךְ אַתָּה, יְיָ אֱלֹהֵינוּ, מֶלֶךְ הָעוֹלָם, בּוֹרֵא פְּרִי הַגָּפֶן.
2. בָּרוּךְ אַתָּה, יְיָ אֱלֹהֵינוּ, מֶלֶךְ הָעוֹלָם, אֲשֶׁר קִדְּשָׁנוּ
3. בְּמִצְוֹתָיו וְרָצָה בָנוּ, וְשַׁבַּת קָדְשׁוֹ בְּאַהֲבָה וּבְרָצוֹן
4. הִנְחִילָנוּ, זִכָּרוֹן לְמַעֲשֵׂה בְרֵאשִׁית. כִּי הוּא יוֹם תְּחִלָּה
5. לְמִקְרָאֵי קֹדֶשׁ, זֵכֶר לִיצִיאַת מִצְרָיִם. כִּי בָנוּ בָחַרְתָּ
6. וְאוֹתָנוּ קִדַּשְׁתָּ מִכָּל הָעַמִּים, וְשַׁבַּת קָדְשְׁךָ בְּאַהֲבָה
7. וּבְרָצוֹן הִנְחַלְתָּנוּ. בָּרוּךְ אַתָּה יְיָ, מְקַדֵּשׁ הַשַּׁבָּת.

Praised are You, Adonai our God, Ruler of the world, who creates the fruit of the vine.
Praised are You, Adonai our God, Ruler of the world, who makes us holy
with commandments and takes delight in us. In God's love and favor God has made the
holy Sabbath our heritage, as a memory of the work of creation.
It is first among our holy days, a memory of the going out from Egypt.
You chose us from all the nations and You made us holy, and in (with) love and favor You
have given us the Sabbath as a sacred inheritance.
Praised are You, Adonai, who makes the Sabbath holy.

<table>
<tr><td>

PRAYER DICTIONARY

קָדוּשׁ
sanctification

זִכָּרוֹן
memory

(לְ)מַעֲשֵׂה בְרֵאשִׁית
work of creation

זֵכֶר
memory

(לִ)יצִיאַת מִצְרַיִם
going out from Egypt

בְּאַהֲבָה
in (with) love

וּבְרָצוֹן
and in (with) favor

</td><td>

WORD CHECK

Put a ✔ next to the Hebrew word that means the same as the English.

1. memory
   - ☐ אַהֲבָה
   - ☐ זִכָּרוֹן

2. and in (with) favor
   - ☐ וּבְרָצוֹן
   - ☐ וְרָצָה

3. memory
   - ☐ זֵכֶר
   - ☐ מִצְרַיִם

4. sanctification
   - ☐ קָדוּשׁ
   - ☐ בָּרוּךְ

5. work of creation
   - ☐ נֵר שֶׁל שַׁבָּת
   - ☐ מַעֲשֵׂה בְרֵאשִׁית

6. in (with) love
   - ☐ בְּאַהֲבָה
   - ☐ בְּרֵאשִׁית

7. going out from Egypt
   - ☐ לְעוֹלָם וָעֶד
   - ☐ יְצִיאַת מִצְרַיִם

</td></tr>
</table>

87

Prayer Building Blocks

קִדּוּשׁ "sanctification"

We know that the root letters קדשׁ mean "holy."

קִדּוּשׁ means "sanctification"
(the act of making something holy)

קִדּוּשׁ helps make שַׁבָּת holy.

The following words all appear in the Kiddush.

Circle the three root letters in each word. Read the words aloud.

מְקַדֵּשׁ קָדְשְׁךָ קִדַּשְׁתָּ קֹדֶשׁ קָדְשׁוֹ קִדְּשָׁנוּ

Read the following lines, and circle the words built on the root קדשׁ.

1. וְשַׁבַּת קָדְשׁוֹ בְּאַהֲבָה וּבְרָצוֹן הִנְחִילָנוּ

2. נְקַדֵּשׁ אֶת שִׁמְךָ בָּעוֹלָם כְּשֵׁם שֶׁמַּקְדִּישִׁים אוֹתוֹ

3. וַיְבָרֶךְ אֱלֹהִים אֶת יוֹם הַשְּׁבִיעִי וַיְקַדֵּשׁ אֹתוֹ

4. קָדוֹשׁ קָדוֹשׁ קָדוֹשׁ יְיָ צְבָאוֹת

5. אַתָּה קִדַּשְׁתָּ אֶת יוֹם הַשְּׁבִיעִי לִשְׁמֶךָ

Put a ✔ next to the ways we can add holiness to our lives.

____ lighting Shabbat candles   ____ watching television

____ watching a golden sunset   ____ baking brownies for a sick friend

____ studying the Torah   ____ going to the mall

Can you add one more example of your own?

_____

88

IMAGINE THAT

The reason the קִדּוּשׁ begins with a blessing over wine may be because in olden times, the drinking of wine was thought of as regal or royal. Starting with this taste of royalty adds a touch of even greater honor and specialness to our celebration.

The cup of wine used for Kiddush is usually filled right to the top. This is to show that our happiness is brimming over as we bless יְיָ. We hope that our lives will overflow with good things.

Think About This!

The Jews are members of a "holy nation." Each and every one of us has the potential to be holy. Fulfilling mitzvot can add holiness to our lives. What do you think "being holy" means?

Prayer Building Blocks

זִכָּרוֹן, זֵכֶר   "memory," "remembrance"

The קִדּוּשׁ recited on שַׁבָּת helps us *remember* why we celebrate שַׁבָּת and make it holy.

The letters זכר tell us that "remember" is part of a word's meaning.

זִכָּרוֹן   means "memory" or "remembrance."

זֵכֶר   also means "memory" or "remembrance."

What three letters are in both זֵכֶר and זִכָּרוֹן? ___ ___ ___

The קָדּוֹשׁ helps us remember events in our history that are reasons for joy.
One reason for joy is mentioned in these words from the קָדּוֹשׁ.

זִכָּרוֹן לְמַעֲשֵׂה בְרֵאשִׁית

remembrance of the work of creation

Circle the Hebrew word that means "memory" or "remembrance."

· ·

Another reason for joy is found in the following words from the קָדּוֹשׁ prayer.

זֵכֶר לִיצִיאַת מִצְרָיִם

memory of the going out from Egypt

Circle the Hebrew word that means "memory" or "remembrance."

· ·

Which three letters tell us that "remember" is part of a word's meaning?

_____ _____ _____

Read the following sentences and circle the words built on the root זכר.

1. וַיֹּאמֶר מֹשֶׁה אֶל הָעָם, זָכוֹר אֶת הַיּוֹם הַזֶּה.

2. בָּרוּךְ אַתָּה, יְיָ אֱלֹהֵינוּ, מֶלֶךְ הָעוֹלָם, זוֹכֵר הַבְּרִית,
   וְנֶאֱמָן בִּבְרִיתוֹ וְקַיָּם בְּמַאֲמָרוֹ.

3. מְקַדֵּשׁ יִשְׂרָאֵל וְיוֹם הַזִּכָּרוֹן.

4. לְמַעַן תִּזְכְּרוּ וַעֲשִׂיתֶם אֶת כָּל מִצְוֹתַי, וִהְיִיתֶם
   קְדשִׁים לֵאלֹהֵיכֶם.

5. וּזְכַרְתֶּם אֶת כָּל מִצְוֹת יְיָ וַעֲשִׂיתֶם אֹתָם.

90

THE HOLIDAY CONNECTION

There is a special day in the Jewish year when we remember all the brave soldiers who died in Israel's wars. We call this day יוֹם הַזִּכָּרוֹן, the Day of Remembrance. יוֹם הַזִּכָּרוֹן is observed in Israel on the day before יוֹם הָעַצְמָאוּת, Israel's Independence Day.

Why do you think the solemn יוֹם הַזִּכָּרוֹן is observed one day before the joyous Day of Independence?

_____

_____

_____

91

Prayer Building Blocks

(לְ)מַעֲשֵׂה בְרֵאשִׁית "work of creation"

When we say קָדוֹשׁ we remember two important events. One of them is the creation of the world.

מַעֲשֵׂה   means "work of."

בְרֵאשִׁית   means "creation" (in the beginning).

בְרֵאשִׁית   is also the Hebrew name for Genesis, the first book of the תּוֹרָה.

Which of the following is not a meaning of בְּרֵאשִׁית? Circle it.

creation   Torah   Genesis   in the beginning

Draw a circle around the Hebrew word that means "the work of."

זִכָּרוֹן לְמַעֲשֵׂה בְרֵאשִׁית

Now draw a star above the Hebrew word that means "creation."

(לְ)יְצִיאַת מִצְרָיִם "going out from Egypt"

The second important event we remember in the קָדוֹשׁ is the *going out from Egypt.*

יְצִיאַת   means "going out from."

מִצְרָיִם   means "Egypt."

Draw a circle around the Hebrew word that means "going out from."

זֵכֶר לִיצִיאַת מִצְרָיִם

Now draw a star above the Hebrew word that means "Egypt."

בְּאַהֲבָה "in (with) love"

בְּאַהֲבָה means "in (with) love."

בְּאַהֲבָה is made up of two parts:

בְּ at the beginning of a word means "in" or "with."

אַהֲבָה means "love."

Circle the prefix that means "in" or "with" in the following Hebrew word.

בְּאַהֲבָה

To the following prefix, add the Hebrew word meaning "love."

בְּ _____

וּבְרָצוֹן "and in (with) favor"

וּבְרָצוֹן means "and in (with) favor."

וּבְרָצוֹן is made up of three parts:

וּ means "and."

בְ at the beginning of a word means "in" or "with."

רָצוֹן means "favor."

Circle the prefix that means "and" in the following Hebrew word.

וּבְרָצוֹן

To the following prefixes, add the Hebrew word meaning "favor."

וּבְ _____

DID YOU KNOW?

The leader of the service recites the קִדּוּשׁ at the end of Friday evening services and we say the קִדּוּשׁ at home before our Shabbat meal.

Why is the קִדּוּשׁ said *twice* on a Friday evening?

The custom of saying the קִדּוּשׁ both at home and in the synagogue began almost 2,000 years ago. Travelers who were far from their homes were often fed and sheltered in the synagogue. To ensure that these people heard the קִדּוּשׁ, the leader of the service recited it in the synagogue for all to hear.

One glass of wine in the synagogue allows all the people there to fulfill the mitzvah of saying the קִדּוּשׁ.

Practice reading the lines below.

1. וַיְכֻלּוּ הַשָּׁמַיִם וְהָאָרֶץ וְכָל צְבָאָם.

2. וַיְבָרֶךְ אֱלֹהִים אֶת יוֹם הַשְּׁבִיעִי וַיְקַדֵּשׁ אֹתוֹ.

3. וּמֵבִיא גוֹאֵל לִבְנֵי בְנֵיהֶם, לְמַעַן שְׁמוֹ, בְּאַהֲבָה.

4. עֲבָדִים הָיִינוּ לְפַרְעֹה בְּמִצְרָיִם.

5. אַתָּה קִדַּשְׁתָּ אֶת יוֹם הַשְּׁבִיעִי לִשְׁמֶךָ.

6. לִבְנֵי יִשְׂרָאֵל עַם קְרֹבוֹ, הַלְלוּיָהּ!

7. זָכוֹר אֶת יוֹם הַשַּׁבָּת לְקַדְּשׁוֹ.

8. אִלּוּ הוֹצִיאָנוּ מִמִּצְרַיִם וְלֹא קָרַע לָנוּ אֶת הַיָּם–דַּיֵּנוּ!

9. בָּרוּךְ אַתָּה, יְיָ אֱלֹהֵינוּ, מֶלֶךְ הָעוֹלָם, אֲשֶׁר בָּחַר בָּנוּ
מִכָּל הָעַמִּים וְנָתַן לָנוּ אֶת תּוֹרָתוֹ.

מִלּוֹן

י	יִמְלֹךְ	will rule	**א**	אוֹר	light
	יִשְׂרָאֵל	Israel		אֶחָד	one
כ	כְּבוֹד	glory of		אֲכִילַת	eating (of)
	כָּמְכָה, כָּמֹכָה	like you		אֱלֹהֵינוּ	our God
				אֲשֶׁר	who
ל	לְאוֹת	as a sign		אַתָּה	you
	לְבָבְךָ	your heart	**ב**	בְּאַהֲבָה	in (with) love
	לְהַדְלִיק	to light		בָּאֵלִם	among the gods
	לֶחֶם	bread			[other nations worship]
	(לְ)יְצִיאַת מִצְרַיִם	going out from Egypt		בּוֹרֵא	who creates
	(לְ)מַעֲשֵׂה בְרֵאשִׁית	work of creation		(בַּ)זְמַן הַזֶּה	at this season, at this time
	לְעוֹלָם וָעֶד	forever and ever		בֵּיתֶךָ	your house
				בְּמִצְוֹתָיו	with God's commandments
מ	מְזוּזוֹת	mezuzot		בַּסֻּכָּה	in the sukkah
	מִי	who		בַּקֹּדֶשׁ	in (the) holiness
	מֶלֶךְ	ruler		בָּרוּךְ	praised, blessed
	מַלְכוּתוֹ	God's kingdom		בָּרְכוּ	praise!
	מִן	from			
	מַעֲרִיב עֲרָבִים	brings on the evening	**ה**	הָאֲדָמָה	the earth
	מַצָּה	matzah		הָאָרֶץ	the earth
	מָרוֹר	maror, bitter herbs		הַגֶּפֶן	the vine
				הַדְּבָרִים	the words
נ	נֶאְדָּר	majestic		הַכֹּל	all things, everything
	נִסִּים	miracles		הַמְבֹרָךְ	who is to be praised
	נֵר	a light, candle		הַמּוֹצִיא	who brings forth
				הָעוֹלָם	the world
ע	עֵץ	tree			
	עֹשֶׂה	makes	**ו**	וְאָהַבְתָּ	you shall love
				וּבוֹרֵא	and creates
פ	פְּרִי	fruit, (the) fruit (of)		וּבְרָצוֹן	and in (with) favor
				וְצִוָּנוּ	and commands us
ק	קִדּוּשׁ	sanctification		וְקַיָּם	and eternal
	קִדְּשָׁנוּ	makes us holy			
			ז	זֵכֶר	memory
שׁ	שַׁבָּת	Shabbat		זִכָּרוֹן	memory
	שֶׁהֶחֱיָנוּ	who has given us life			
	שׁוֹפָר	shofar	**ח**	חַי	living, lives
	שֶׁל	of		חֲנֻכָּה	Hanukkah
	שָׁלוֹם	peace		חֹשֶׁךְ	darkness
	שֵׁם	name			
	שְׁמַע	hear	**י**	יוֹצֵר	forms
				יְיָ	Adonai